The UNOFFICIAL GUIDE *to*

Even More of Hockey's Most Unusual Records

The **Unofficial Guide** to
EVEN MORE OF
HOCKEY'S
MOST UNUSUAL
Don Weekes & Kerry Banks
RECORDS

GREYSTONE BOOKS

Douglas & McIntyre Publishing Group
Vancouver/Toronto/Berkeley

To the future of our game.

Greystone Books
A division of Douglas & McIntyre Ltd.
2323 Quebec Street, Suite 201
Vancouver, British Columbia
Canada V5T 4S7
www.greystonebooks.com

Library and Archives Canada Cataloguing in Publication
Weekes, Don
  The unofficial guide to even more of hockey's most unusual records /
  Don Weekes & Kerry Banks

  Includes index.
  ISBN 1-55365-062-X

  1. National Hockey League—Miscellanea. 2. Hockey—Miscellanea.
I. Banks, Kerry, 1952– II. Title.
GV847.W44185 2004   796.962'64   C2004-903374-3

Library of Congress Cataloguing-in-Publication Data
Weekes, Don
  The unofficial guide to even more of hockey's most unusual records /
  Don Weekes & Kerry Banks
  p. cm.
  Includes index.
  ISBN 1-55365-062-X (trade paper : alk. paper)
  1. National Hockey League—Miscellanea. 2. Hockey—Miscellanea. 3. Hockey—Records.
I. Banks, Kerry, 1952– II. Title.
GV847.8.N3W45 2004
796.962'64—dc22   2004054363

Editing by Anne Rose
Cover design by Peter Cocking & Jessica Sullivan
Cover photograph by Bruce Bennett/Bruce Bennett Studios
Interior design by Peter Cocking
Typeset by Bonne Zabolotney
Printed and bound in Canada by Friesens
Printed on acid-free paper that is forest friendly (100% post-consumer recyled paper)
and has been processed chlorine free.
Distributed in the U.S. by Publishers Group West

We gratefully acknowledge the financial support of the Canada Council for the Arts,
the British Columbia Arts Council, and the Government of Canada through the Book
Publishing Industry Development Program (BPIDP) for our publishing activities.

Contents

Introduction

The word "deke" has never received its proper due. Although not considered dictionary-worthy, watch a game and there it is, a standard of play-by-play—used when a player fakes out an opponent. Frankly, this slice of hockey slang (from the word decoy) typifies the spirit of the *Unofficial Guide* series. We are drawn to the curious and offbeat stuff that distinguishes our game. Even better, we treasure material mined from the extraordinary.

What qualifies as an unusual hockey record? The definition is fluid. Some hit you in the face, like Randy Exelby, a guy few have heard of but who holds a record no other goalie can claim. Exelby made his NHL debut in relief of Patrick Roy, when Roy had to take a bathroom break during a game in 1989. That's definitely unusual and that's definitely in this book, as is the most horrifying injury suffered by a superstar, the only dog to get its name engraved on the Stanley Cup, the only NHLer banned from playing games in another city and the first goalie to try to sell advertising space on his pads.

An unofficial record is a little different—it could be a legitimate record that the NHL does not officially acknowledge, such as best regular-season power-play scoring percentage by a team. (The most deadly squad was the Guy Lafleur-led Montreal Canadiens, with a 31.9 per cent efficiency rate in 1977–78.)

Unofficial can also mean ignored, like the 32 games mysteriously missing from King Clancy's Maple Leaf coaching record. The NHL credits the winning and losing of those games to other Toronto coaches, who were in hospital beds at the time. Presumably, they were changing lines by telepathy.

An unofficial record can also be the never-seen-before record, uncovered by our original research, such as the first NHLer to score an empty-net goal. We believe it's Cecil Dillon of the New York Rangers, and that he did it in on January 12, 1932.

Sure, we're deking around some hallowed traditions, but we're also honouring the game too. Wayne, Gordie, Bobby, Mario and the Rocket all get their due—both the good, the bad and the ugly. And that's the way it should be.

DON WEEKES & KERRY BANKS
March 2004

CHAPTER 1

Taking
flight

History changed when a hockey stick struck the face of Wilbur Wright. Seventeen years before he and brother Orville flew their first plane, Wilbur lost some teeth in a game of shinny. During his recovery, he read extensively. "The hockey accident set the stage that led to his intense interest in flight," says Dawne Dewey, historian at Wright State University. Here are some other groundbreaking records.

Most unbreakable NHL record

Consecutive complete games by a goalie, career
502: Glenn Hall, October 6, 1955 to November 7, 1962

Hall's ironman streak defined gut-check, literally. He puked before each of his record 502 contests. *Sports Illustrated* hailed Hall's endurance mark (for appearances, not throw-ups), describing it as "the record of records, a mark we will swear, on the good book of *Guinness,* won't ever be broken" in all of sports.

Most unbreakable NHL scoring record by two teams
Fastest two goals, both teams
2 seconds: St. Louis vs. Boston, December 19, 1987

Sound impossible? It happened. With Boston trailing St. Louis 6–4 and goalie Doug Keans pulled for a sixth attacker, Ken Linseman scored at 19:50. With nothing to lose, the Bruins left Keans on the bench for the centre-ice faceoff. When the puck was dropped, Blues centre Doug Gilmour drilled it down the ice and into the open cage to seal a 7–5 win. The elapsed time was two seconds.

Most unbreakable NHL record by one team

Winning percentage, one season
.875: Boston Bruins, 1929–30

This record may be a product of an era, but only one team, Boston, exploited the NHL's new rule on forward passing in 1929–30 to set a standard not since broken. The Bruins' 38–5–1 record earned 77 of a possible 88 points in the 44-game schedule, a .875 winning percentage. Even in today's game, where teams can boost point totals with overtime losses, a club would still have to finish the season with 144 of a potential 164 points to break Boston's mark.

Most embarrassing NHL goalie record

Losses by a goalie, one season
48: Gary Smith, California Golden Seals, 1970–71

The NHL hates to highlight negative aspects of records. For example, Detroit owns the official mark for most consecutive goals in one game, 15, in a 15–0 massacre of the New York Rangers in January 1944. But the NHL *Official Guide and Record Book* lists no corresponding team or individual record for goals-against, saving the Rangers and their shell-shocked goalie, Ken McAuley, serious face in the history books. To be fair, the *Guide* does include a few embarrassments, such as team losing streaks and penalties, though the best may be its register of goalies with the most regular-season defeats. California's Gary Smith heads this desperate group with 48 losses in 1970–71.

Most embarrassing unofficial goalie record

Goals allowed, one game
16: Frank Brophy, Quebec Bulldogs, March 3, 1920

Brophy can rest in peace since there is no official individual NHL record detailing his 16-goal ordeal at the hands of the Montreal Canadiens. The besieged Bulldogs goalie played 20 more games in 1919–20 and was ventilated for another 132 goals.

Most embarrassing NHL records by a team

Fewest wins, one season (min. 70 games)
8: Washington Capitals, 1974–75
Most games shut out, one season
20: Chicago Blackhawks, 1928–29

The expansion Capitals had a good excuse for their first-year disaster, but can you imagine how bad it got on the bench with just eight wins all season? Their 8–67–5 record was the tip of the iceberg, concealing an underbelly of equally humiliating NHL records, such as most goals-against and fewest points by a team. Equally pathetic, in 1928–29's 44-game schedule, Chicago was shut out in almost half of its games. The helpless Hawks were blanked in 20 matches, including a record eight straight in February 1929. All told, Chicago didn't score for more than 550 consecutive minutes.

Most unsportsmanlike conduct by a losing team
Montreal Canadiens, April 16, 1954
A lot of bench-clearing brawls have bloodied the game, but the 1954 Stanley Cup finals featured a one-of-a-kind ending that brought new meaning to unsportsmanlike play. Not a punch was thrown nor a stick swung in vengeance. Deadlocked 1–1 in overtime in Game 7, Detroit's Tony Leswick scored on a screen shot that deflected off Doug Harvey's glove and past goalie Gerry McNeil. A cheap goal won the Cup before a delirious crowd in Detroit, and the Canadiens petulantly skated off the ice before the customary handshakes with the Red Wings.

Most height involved in a fight
13 feet, four inches: Zdeno Chara, Ottawa, and Hal Gill, Boston
The two biggest players in NHL history, six-foot-nine Zdeno Chara and six-foot-seven Hal Gill, have fought one another twice so far in their careers. The first bout was in 2002–03 and the second in 2003–04. At least no one can accuse them of being afraid to pick on someone their own size.

Most humiliating injuries sustained from underestimating an opponent in a fight
Lou Fontinato, New York Rangers, February 1, 1959
Once considered the NHL's premier pugilist, Fontinato made the career-altering mistake of trading blows with Gordie Howe. The

big Red Wing hadn't dropped the gloves in years and Fontinato smelled an easy knockdown. But Fontinato's initial flurry of punches only woke a sleeping giant. Howe shook off the jabs, grabbed the neck of his tormentor's jersey and repeatedly drove his right fist into Fontinato's face. By the time Howe was done, the Ranger rearguard's nose and cheekbone had been mashed to a bloody pulp. Only plastic surgery could repair the damage. To add insult to injury, pictures of the fight and Fontinato's battered mug ran in *Life* magazine. Leapin' Lou never skated with the same strut again.

Most "front teeth" knocked out, career
12: Ken Daneyko, New Jersey, 1983–84 to 2002–03
During his playing career, Daneyko wore dental bridges with false teeth to fill the many holes in his mouth. But after his retirement in 2003, he became a smiling example of cosmetic dental surgery—with porcelain implants and permanent bridges to replace the seven upper and five lower teeth he lost to high sticks, flying pucks and punches. Unofficially, Daneyko knew the tooth fairy better than anyone.

Most pucks to hit one family, one game
2: Mr. and Mrs. Lou Reese, March 28, 1943
It was a busy night in the Red Wings' infirmary—not for injured players, but for the fans in attendance. First up was Mrs. Reese, who took four stitches after being struck in the face by a puck. Then, moments after she returned to her seat, another stray puck cut her husband and sent him to the clinic for two stitches. Those who were watching the game saw the Wings beat Toronto 4–2.

Most costly misconduct penalty

Eddie Shore, Boston, March 26, 1936

Shore's legendary temper cost the Bruins big time during the 1936 playoffs. The Bruins and the Leafs were playing the second of a two-game total-goal series in Toronto. Boston had won the first game 3–0, and, with the two clubs tied 1–1 in the second period of Game 2, looked well on its way to advancing to the next round. But Shore was becoming increasingly agitated by the calls of referee Odie Cleghorn. And when Red Horner scored a disputed goal to put the Leafs up 2–1, Shore and Cleghorn had words. The ref gave him two minutes for delaying the game. Shore then retrieved the puck and flipped it off Cleghorn's hindquarters, earning himself a 10-minute misconduct. With its star defenseman in the box, Boston collapsed and Toronto rolled to an 8–3 victory, taking the series on total goals, 8–6.

Most costly too-many-men-on-the-ice penalty
Boston Bruins, May 10, 1979

Leading Montreal 4–3 with 2:34 left in the third period of Game 7 of the semifinals, the Bruins were whistled for too many men on the ice. Guy Lafleur rifled a slapper past goalie Gilles Gilbert on the ensuing power play, tying the game, and the Habs went on to win the series in overtime on a goal by Yvon Lambert. The costly penalty did nothing to ease coach Don Cherry's stormy relationship with GM Harry Sinden, and contributed to Cherry's firing a few months later.

Most costly use of an illegal stick

Marty McSorley, Los Angeles, June 3, 1993

McSorley was penalized for using a stick with an illegal curve with less than two minutes left in Game 2 of the 1993 finals against Montreal. Until that point, the visiting Kings, who led the game 2–1 and the series 1–0, looked to be on the Stanley Cup expressway. The Habs scored on the resulting power play, sending the contest into overtime. Montreal defenseman Eric Desjardins netted the winner 51 seconds into sudden death, and the revitalized Canadiens went on to capture the Cup in five games. Why a stone-handed plumber like McSorley would be using a stick with a major curve is anyone's guess, but the gaffe proved to be the turning point in the series.

Most costly autograph

US$1,000: Tie Domi, Toronto, February 11, 2004
Players don't often pay money for signing memorabilia, but a little showmanship with an autographed stick cost Domi a chunk of cash. After mixing it up all game with Columbus forward Jody Shelley, Domi pulled out a pen while sitting on the Maple Leafs bench, signed his stick and chucked it over the glass partition between the benches toward Shelley. Domi got a US$1,000 fine for stick swinging (a slight stretch of the rule), and the Leafs had to fork over a US$5,000 fine.

Longest NHL game

176:30 minutes: Detroit vs. Montreal Maroons, March 24–25, 1936
There has never been a match to rival the epic Red Wings-Maroons clash of March 1936. A capacity crowd of 9,000 fans jammed the Montreal Forum through three scoreless periods. Then, the real marathon began. Almost six extra periods later, only a few thousand diehards remained to witness Detroit's Mud Bruneteau score the winner on goalie Lorne Chabot. With no mechanized ice-cleaning equipment, the bone-weary players were practically skating on snow by game's end. Still, the teams combined for 159 shots, as the Wings' Normie Smith

faced 92 and Chabot gave up Bruneteau's goal on his 67th shot on net. Mercifully, the match ended at 2:25 AM, after almost six hours of play.

Longest time span between NHL games at one arena
32 years: St. Louis Arena, March 12, 1935 to October 11, 1967
When the old Ottawa Senators folded after the 1933–34 season, the franchise moved to St. Louis. The Eagles, as the team was known, became the first NHL club established west of the Mississippi—though the last-place Eagles lasted only one year. When the NHL returned to St. Louis 32 years later, the Blues took up residence in the Eagles' former home, the St. Louis Arena.

Most different arenas with the same name
4: Madison Square Garden
There have been four different Madison Square Gardens. The first was built in 1874, the second in 1890 on the same site, the third in 1925 at a different location and the fourth in 1968 on the same site as the third.

Most NHL teams based at the same arena
2: Montreal Forum, Montreal Maroons and Montreal Canadiens
2: Madison Square Garden, NY Rangers and NY Americans
They were good situations for developing a rivalry, but in the long run, these "housing" arrangements were not so good for the economic health of the Maroons and the Americans. Both teams ultimately lost out in the popularity race and folded. The Maroons and the Canadiens shared the Montreal Forum from 1926–27 to 1937–38. The Rangers and the Americans were co-tenants at Madison Square Garden from 1926–27 to 1941–42.

Most arenas in one country

3,350: Canada

Canadians may not dominate the NHL like they once did, but when it comes to indoor rinks, Canada is top dog, with a huge lead: more than a half-million registered players playing on 3,350 indoor rinks. The US supports 2,500 rinks, and Russia, surprisingly, fewer than 100.

Largest hockey sweater ever made

Size 360: Detroit Red Wings, 1997

To cheer on the Red Wings during their 1997 Stanley Cup run, employees of East Side Team Sports in Warren, Michigan, dressed the muscular shoulders of the Spirit of Detroit statue in a giant Detroit jersey. The statue outside the City County building required a size 360—considered the largest sweater ever made.

Most difficult name to fit on a sweater

John Brackenborough, Boston, 1925–26

In addition to having the longest surname of any NHLer (14 letters), Brackenborough is noteworthy for another reason. On February 29, 1924, during a senior league game, the centre was struck in the face by an errant stick and lost his right eye. Despite the injury, Brackenborough later resumed his career and played seven games with the Boston Bruins in 1925–26. The Bruins supposedly cut Brackenborough when they realized he was blind in one eye. Still, at least Boston didn't have to worry about sewing Brackenborough's name on a sweater: the Bruins didn't adopt the concept for another 50 years.

Most prominent hockey names joined in matrimony
The Morenz and Geoffrion families, 1952
She was the figure skating daughter of the legendary Howie
Morenz. He was the future Hall of Fame sniper of the Montreal
Canadiens. So when bluebloods Marlene Morenz and Bernie
Geoffrion united two generations of the Canadiens, it was a
match made in ice heaven. The two had met at a Montreal
Forum skating event where Marlene was a professional skater.
Halfway through her routine, she slipped on a paper-cup lid and
tumbled across the ice, landing flat on her tush directly in front
of Geoffrion, who was in attendance as part of a promotion with
the Canadiens. When Marlene looked up in humiliation, there
was Geoffrion, with a smirk on his face and a twinkle in his eye.
The couple was introduced after the show and wed that spring.

Most unknown hockey superstar
Hobey Baker, Princeton, 1910s
Most of us have no idea who Hobey Baker is. Beyond the trophy
dedicated in his honour (which goes to the US college hockey
player of the year), even hockey aficionados say, "Hobey who"?
Baker was equal parts legend, myth and hero. In his Princeton
University days, he starred at everything he tried, but, limited by
the rules to two varsity sports, his fields of dreams were football
and hockey. It was reported that Baker, an exceptional skater
and stickhandler, after once being checked over the boards,
dashed along the bench, leapt back into action, got the loose
puck and scored. Some say his heroics were so amazing, they
sound like fantasy. Although he never played in the NHL, he
captained Princeton to two intercollegiate championships,
the equivalent of national titles. In one year alone he scored
92 points, his school's single-season record for the next 62 years.
Baker, who flew with the famous Escadrille Lafayette in World

War I, arrived too late for most of the air war, but recorded three kills. He died in a crash a few days after the armistice was signed.

Most important item not in the Hockey Hall of Fame
Canada-USSR Summit Series-winning puck, 1972
For many Canadians, Paul Henderson's winning goal at the 1972 Summit Series stands as hockey's greatest moment. But whatever happened to the puck? Its whereabouts are known to only three men: Henderson and teammates Pat Stapleton and Bill White. Video of the celebrated goal shows Henderson being mobbed by teammates as Stapleton retrieves the puck. Henderson maintains he doesn't have it but would like it in the Hall of Fame. Stapleton and White each claim it's in the other's possession. Why all the secrecy? "Once we disclose where it is, the mystery is gone and we've got nothing to talk about," White said in November 2000.

Most treasonous act in international competition
Jacques Plante, 1972
He probably did it out of sympathy for a fellow goalie facing overwhelming odds, but Plante must have had a few regrets after the Soviets humiliated Canada 7–3 in the opening game of the 1972 Summit Series. It is well known today that before Game 1, Vladislav Tretiak received a surprise visit from Plante, who, through the aid of a translator and blackboard diagrams, instructed the young Soviet netminder on how to stop Canada's top marksmen. The loss exposed Canada's biggest weakness. It wasn't its Benedict Arnold, but lack of preparation, particularly in properly assessing Soviet strengths such as Tretiak.

Most important historical hockey issue in dispute

The birthplace of hockey

Is it Montreal, Kingston, Halifax or Windsor, Nova Scotia? Unlike other sports, hockey is still trying to decide where it was born. It has turned into a good fight—one many feel will go on forever, given the disputes over the definition of the game. Various historical references, from diaries and sketches dating back to 1825, depict men with crude sticks skating on frozen surfaces, but should that be considered the Canadian game of organized hockey? Or is it shinny or hurley, European games brought to North America centuries ago? Montreal claims to have hosted the first documented game with rules on March 3, 1875. Halifax disputes this, insisting that even though a McGill student, James Creighton, may have started hockey in Montreal, he came from Halifax, where the game was already being played.

CHAPTER 2

Numerology

Ever since Wayne Gretzky sported jersey No. 99 in 1979–80, it has been open season on sweater numbers. Thankfully, NHL regulations bar three-digit numbers, numbers with fractions and decimal points. No. 00 is also banned. Within these parameters, players adopt numbers for different reasons. Some don't care, while others exhibit an occult-like faith in the numerals plastered on their backs.

Most respected sweater number in hockey
9
Maurice Richard, Gordie Howe and Bobby Hull made No. 9 hockey's most famous number. Wayne Gretzky later paid his own tribute by doubling the digit, but the greatest compliment may be when a lesser player recognizes the significance of No. 9 and chooses something else.

First signature number in hockey
99: Wayne Gretzky, 1979–80 to 1998–99
No self-respecting player could wear this number today and still look himself in the mirror. Still, a few tried (Wilf Paiement and Rick Dudley) early in Gretzky's career—before he became a living legend and before the No. 99 was retired league-wide in 1999.

First player to wear No. 99
Joe Lamb, Montreal, 1934–35
More than 40 years before Wayne Gretzky played his first NHL game, the Montreal Canadiens assigned No. 99 to Joe Lamb, whom they had just acquired from Boston for Johnny "Black Cat" Gagnon. It was like painting a bull's eye on Lamb's back. The hardrock winger, who was already disliked for his involvement in several vicious muggings of Montreal players in his two previous years with the Bruins, didn't win many converts. Three weeks later, the Habs returned Lamb to Boston for cash.

First non-goalie to wear No. I on an NHL team
Herb Gardiner, Montreal, 1926–27
Breaking with hockey tradition, Gardiner, a defenseman, wore

No. 1 with Montreal after goalie great Georges Vezina collapsed during a game and died of tuberculosis in 1926. Considering whom they were replacing and the tragedy surrounding his death, no goalie touched the number until George Hainsworth made it his own four years later. Gardiner wasn't the only non-goalie on the Canadiens with No. 1, however. After Gardiner's trade in 1928, D-man Marty Burke took the numeral and, later, Babe Seibert wore No. 1 for Montreal in the 1930s.

Only modern-era players to wear the same number on the same team, one season

Robbie Ftorek and Claude Larose, WHA Cincinnati Stingers, 1977–78

We don't believe it has ever happened in modern-day NHL action, but when Ftorek and Larose both wanted the same number, Cincinnati received special permission from the WHA's head office so that each player could sport No. 8. It must have been hell on the scorekeepers.

Most disastrous sweater number assignment

Bobby Hull's No. 9 to Dave Tallon, Chicago Blackhawks, 1973–74

As a Canuck, Tallon was the toast of Vancouver after scoring 56 points to set a rookie record for defense in 1970–71. Two years later, he was rudely booed and the target of a public outcry in Chicago when the club assigned him Hull's famous No. 9. It was a stupid move by management, still sore over the Golden Jet's departure to the rival WHA the previous season. But it was Tallon's popularity that took a big hit, and it didn't help him cope with the already high-pressure expectations heaped on him. In the end, Tallon wore No. 9 for only part of the Blackhawks' 1973 training camp and in one preseason game.

First player to have his number retired

Ace Bailey, Toronto, February 14, 1934

Bailey's career was violently terminated on December 12, 1933, when he was hit from behind by Eddie Shore of the Boston Bruins and suffered a fractured skull. Two months later, Bailey's former club hosted a team of All-Stars in an exhibition game, with the proceeds going to Bailey and his family. Shore was named a member of the All-Star team, but tensions quickly passed when Bailey shook Shore's hand in forgiveness. Leafs owner Conn Smythe retired the first number in hockey history when he declared of Bailey's No. 6: "No other player will ever use this number on the Maple Leaf hockey team." The game was a success for the home side, with Toronto posting a 7–3 victory over Shore, Howie Morenz and their fellow All-Stars.

First player with an unofficially retired number

Larry Aurie, No. 6, Detroit, 1927–28 to 1938–39

They called Aurie "Little Dempsey." Although only five foot six and 148 pounds, he was a fearless competitor, a team leader on Detroit's first two Stanley Cup champions and team owner James Norris's favourite player. When Aurie left the game in 1939, Norris immediately retired his number. But after Norris and Aurie died, things changed. Today, you won't find Aurie's No. 6 among the banners at Joe Louis Arena honouring Detroit's greats. Members of Aurie's family, who asked for an explanation, were told by Wings management that Aurie's number is "unofficially retired." In other words, it's out of circulation but not important enough to hang in the rafters.

First unofficially retired number that was later unretired

Wayne Maki, No. 11, Vancouver, 1997

Maki played three seasons with the Canucks in the early 1970s.

His No. 11 was retired by the club after he suddenly developed brain cancer and died in 1974. The number lay in state until July 1997, when the Canucks' new management group, Orca Bay Entertainment, signed free agent Mark Messier, hockey's most famous No. 11. The Moose requested and received No. 11 and wore it at his first Vancouver press conference. No one from the team thought to call Maki's widow, however, to give her the news. When she protested, the team claimed that Maki's No. 11 had never actually been retired. Instead, it was an "honoured number," which meant that it was a perfect fit for a US$20-million free agent from New York.

First player to wear a sweater number in honour of a New Yankees baseball player

Chris Drury, Buffalo Sabres, 2003–04
Drury was the winning pitcher in the 1989 Little League World Series against Taiwan. Born in Trumbull, Connecticut, his sports heroes included his brother, Ted, who played for the US at the World Juniors, and Yankee first baseman Don Mattingly. When he was traded to Buffalo, Drury took No. 23 in honour of Mattingly.

Most obvious sweater number to honour Wayne Gretzky

66: Mario Lemieux, Pittsburgh, 1984–85 to 2003–04

The inspiration to turn No. 99 upside down came from Lemieux's agent Bob Perno, who suggested No. 66 as a comparison to Gretzky's No. 99. Lemieux wore it first with the Laval Voisins of the Quebec Junior League, in 1981–82. He is the only player to have any success wearing a number inspired by the Great One.

Most patriotic choice of a sweater number

Jaromir Jagr, No. 68, Pittsburgh, 1990

Born in 1972, Jagr chose No. 68 as a way to symbolize his country's struggle for freedom from Communist repression. (In 1968, the Soviet Union invaded Jagr's native Czechoslovakia.) Ironically, Jagr's appearance on draft day in 1990 marked the first time that a Czech player attended an NHL draft without having to defect.

First player to change his number for charity

Brett Hull, Detroit, September 2003

Hull donned No. 80 instead of his usual No. 17 during Detroit's 2003–04 preseason games, in honour of coach Herb Brooks, who was killed in a car crash on August 11, 2003. Hull then autographed the sweaters and donated them to the Brooks family's charitable foundation. Hull chose No. 80 because 1980 was the year that Brooks coached Team U.S.A. to its Miracle on Ice victory at the Olympics. "He was a very, very special person for hockey, not only U.S.A. Hockey, but hockey worldwide," said Hull, who won a silver medal playing for Brooks at the Salt Lake Olympics in 2002.

Only player whose number change was inspired by a condiment

Steve Heinze, Columbus, 2000

Heinze played nine seasons in Boston without succumbing to the urge, but after being scooped up by the Columbus Blue Jackets in the 2000 Expansion Draft, the right-winger did the inevitable and became Heinze 57.

Only player to change his sweater number to celebrate his sobriety

Bob Probert, Chicago, 1997–98

The pugnacious left-winger converted from No. 24 to No. 95 to commemorate the year he changed his life by giving up drugs and alcohol. In 1989, Probert was convicted of smuggling cocaine, and, in 1994, for causing an accident while driving a motorcycle under the influence of cocaine and alcohol. The latter offense resulted in a season-long suspension.

First NHL player to wear No. 13

Gizzy Hart, Detroit Cougars, 1926

The superstitions surrounding No. 13 have made it an extremely unpopular choice for NHLers. Although the history is sketchy, the first to don No. 13 is believed to be Gizzy Hart, a Stanley Cup winner with the 1925 Victoria Cougars and one of the NHL's first Jewish players. Hart reportedly wore the number in a couple of games with the Detroit Cougars early in the 1926–27 season, before being sold to the Canadiens, where he wore No. 11. Nick Wasnie reportedly donned No. 13 briefly for Chicago the following year, but it was not until 1952 that a player wore the number for a full season: winger Jack Stoddard of the New York Rangers.

First player to have his number worn by an entire team during a pre-game warm-up

Bryan Trottier, NY Islanders, October 20, 2001

In what is sure to become an NHL tradition, Trottier's name and No. 19 were worn by the entire Islander team during the pre-game skate. Trottier, the sixth Islander to have his number retired, was further honoured by visiting San Jose Sharks coach Darryl Sutter, who said: "I told Trots that, if 20 years ago I'd seen

20 Bryan Trottiers skating around before the game, I would have just laid down at centre ice."

Only lines nicknamed after their sweater numbers
The Dice Line, Calgary, 1980s
The Crazy Eights, Philadelphia, 1992–93

The Flames' Dice Line took its name from the fact that all three members of the unit, Colin Patterson, Rich Kromm and Carey Wilson, wore double digits: 11, 22 and 33, respectively. The Flyers' Crazy Eights line was composed of Eric Lindros (88), Mark Recchi (8) and Brent Fedyk (18).

Lowest number not retired by a team

13

With so few players wearing unlucky No. 13, it's the only numeral between one and 20 that hasn't been retired by at least one NHL club.

Highest number not retired by a team

98

Of course, with No. 99 gone forever (the NHL retired it league-wide in 1999), the next-highest number available to grace the rafters one day should be No. 98.

Highest number worn by an NHLer since Wayne Gretzky retired

97: Jeremy Roenick, Phoenix, Philadelphia, 1996–97 to 2003–04

Roenick wore No. 27 in Chicago, but after his trade to Phoenix at the 1997 Entry Draft, he switched to No. 97. Roenick was one of about a dozen players who sported sweater numbers in the nineties in 2003-04.

First team to wear high numbers

Montreal Canadiens, 1934–35

In a move designed to divert the attention of irate fans from the preseason trade of legendary Howie Morenz to Chicago, the Canadiens introduced a radical concept in uniform numbers. Several players were assigned digits higher than 40—unheard of in an era when no other team had a number higher than 19. Defensemen Jack Portland and Roger Jenkins wore 75 and 88, respectively. Among the forwards, Paul Raymond donned 48, Jack McGill, 55 and Armand Mondou, 64. Montreal was smart enough to leave Morenz's No. 7 untouched.

Most sweater numbers higher than 40 worn by a team, one season

10: Montreal Canadiens, 2003–04

There is a lot to consider when a player asks for a low number on the Canadiens. Seven digits between one and 16 have been retired and many other unretired numbers have been worn by Montreal Hall of Famers. In fact, the Hall of Fame has inducted far more members of the Canadiens than the club has seen fit to honour with retired jerseys. But that doesn't mean every unretired number is available. As one Montreal trainer said in 2003, "If a player asked for No. 23 (GM Bob Gainey's former number), you can be sure we'll be making a call upstairs." Montreal set the record in 2003–04 with 10 regulars with numerals over 40, including Mike Ribeiro's No. 71, Michael Ryder's No. 73 and Jose Theodore's No. 60.

Most Hall of Fame players from one team whose numbers have not been retired

21: Montreal Canadiens

You would think that Hall of Fame status would guarantee a

number in the rafters, but Montreal, among a very few teams, has stiffer qualifications than the Hall when it comes to honouring players. More than 20 Hall of Famers—inducted because of their play with the Canadiens—have not had their numbers retired by the team. As we went to press, the list included Ken Dryden, Larry Robinson, Bernie Geoffrion, Dickie Moore, Serge Savard, Elmer Lach, Yvan Cournoyer and Jacques Lemaire.

Most numbers retired by one team
10: Boston Bruins, 1924–25 to 2002–03
The Bruins' honour role includes Eddie Shore (2), Lionel Hitchman (3), Bobby Orr (4), Dit Clapper (5), Phil Esposito (7), Cam Neely (8), Johnny Bucyk (9), Milt Schmidt (15), Terry O'Reilly (24) and Ray Bourque (77).

Fewest retired numbers by a team that has existed for 30 years or more
0: New Jersey Devils
The lack of a single retired number indicates just how impoverished a history the Devils have had. For a long time the New Jersey franchise was a ghost ship. But the tide has turned and retired numbers are on the horizon. Who will be the first Devil to have his jersey raised to the rafters? Might it be Ken Daneyko?

Only players to have their numbers retired by an NHL team they never played for
J.C. Tremblay, Quebec Nordiques
John McKenzie, Hartford Whalers
Both Tremblay and McKenzie were multiple Stanley Cup winners before joining the WHA in 1972–73. There, they spent the remainder of their hockey careers playing the entire seven-year term of the WHA, mostly for the Nordiques and Whalers. When

the two clubs joined the NHL in 1979–80, Tremblay's No. 3 and McKenzie's No. 19 were retired, even though neither played a single NHL game as a Nordique or as a Whaler.

Only player whose number was retired because he lost his life in an NHL game
Bill Masterton, Minnesota North Stars, 1967–68
Masterton, who was a member of the North Stars expansion team in 1967–68, died after suffering a skull fracture during a game on January 13, 1968. In his honour, the NHL created the Bill Masterton Memorial Trophy, an annual award given to the player who best exemplifies the qualities of perseverance, sportsmanship and dedication to hockey. Although Masterton's No. 19 was never worn by another North Star, it was not officially retired until 1987.

Most goalie numbers retired by a team in one night
2: Chicago Blackhawks, November 20, 1988
In a two-for-one bonanza, Chicago retired Glenn Hall's No. 1 and Tony Esposito's No. 35 before a game on November 20, 1988. Why Hall's number had not already been honoured before this time is a bit puzzling. Hall and Esposito remain the only goalkeepers to have their numbers retired by the Blackhawks.

Only Canadian province to retire a sweater number
Quebec, 2000
In 2000, Hockey Quebec, the association that represents 90,000 players in the province's minor-hockey development program, announced that teams representing Quebec in national competition could not use No. 9—the number worn by Maurice Richard.

First Major League Baseball club to honour an NHLer by sewing his number on its jerseys

Montreal Expos, 2000

In a unique gesture honouring the late Maurice Richard, the Expos sewed his No. 9 on the right sleeves of their home and away sweaters during the 2000 season. It marked the first time that an athlete from another sport was venerated in this way.

Most stringent policy regarding the retirement of a player's number by a team

Honoured versus retired numbers, Toronto Maple Leafs

Toronto is the only NHL franchise that requires a career-ending injury or a death certificate to retire a player's number. Ace Bailey almost succumbed on the operating table after a brutal hit from Eddie Shore in 1933. He never played again but saw his No. 6 retired. Bill Barilko perished in a plane crash shortly after scoring the Leafs' Stanley Cup-winning goal in 1951. His No. 5 is the last retired Toronto number. The greatest Leaf stars—Charlie Conacher, Syl Apps, Johnny Bower, Tim Horton and so on—are remembered with "honoured" numbers, which doesn't prevent them from being worn.

Heroes
of the hall

Among Bobby Orr's many records is
one he would prefer not to hold:
youngest player inducted into the Hall of Fame. He
was just 30 when he entered the Hall in 1979—
forced into retirement by his failing body. Orr's
knees were his Achilles heel. Multiple surgeries to
repair torn ligaments and loose cartilage spelled a
premature end for the spectacular defenseman.

First active player elected to the Hall of Fame

Dit Clapper, February 12, 1947

Prior to a game against the New York Rangers, the 40-year-old Bruins playing-coach was presented with a scroll signifying his admission into the Hockey Hall of Fame. Clapper was also given a sterling silver tea set as a reward for playing 20 NHL seasons. During the ceremony, Clapper announced his retirement as a player. It was a night of historic happenings. Boston blasted New York 10–1 and Bill Cowley picked up a goal and assist to surpass Syd Howe as the NHL's all-time leading scorer.

First Hall of Famer to have his own Hall of Fame
Bobby Orr, July 18, 2003

A Hall of Fame dedicated to Orr had its grand opening in July 2003, in his hometown of Parry Sound, Ontario. The fabled No. 4 appeared at the event and gave an emotional speech expressing his thanks. The museum includes audio-visual displays, home movies of Orr as a child and assorted memorabilia, including the stick Orr used to score the Stanley Cup-clinching overtime goal in 1970, his original Boston Garden locker, the Cup rings he received from the Bruins after their 1970 and 1972 championships and his original NHL contract. (By the way, that 1966–67 contract paid him US$25,000, a princely sum at the time for a rookie.)

Most inductions into sports Halls of Fame

4: Lionel Conacher, 1925–26 to 1936–37

In 1950, Conacher was voted Canada's athlete of the half-century—with good reason. The man they called the Big Train was an amateur boxing champion, a star performer in lacrosse, baseball, football and track and field—as well as hockey, a sport he didn't take up until he was 16. Conacher, who died of a heart attack while running bases in a charity baseball game in 1954, is a member of four different Halls of Fame: the Canadian Sports Hall of Fame, Canadian Football Hall of Fame, Canadian Lacrosse Hall of Fame and Hockey Hall of Fame.

Most ironic combination of Hall of Fame inductees, one year
Andy Bathgate and Jacques Plante, 1978
Few hockey fans missed the irony of Plante and Bathgate being inducted into the Hall together in 1978. It was Bathgate who, on November 1, 1959, fired the fateful shot that split Plante's nose. After undergoing stitchwork at the Madison Square Garden clinic, Plante returned to the ice wearing a mask. He would wear it for the rest of his career, forever changing the face of hockey.

First European-trained Hall of Famer
Borje Salming, 1973–74 to 1989–90
A trailblazer, Salming was at the forefront of the European invasion, joining the Toronto Maple Leafs in 1973–74. Labelled "Chicken Swede," he persevered through verbal baiting and bullying tactics to play 1,148 games and become one of the NHL's most outstanding defensemen. Salming, who spent 16 years in a Leafs uniform, even earned the respect of Toronto owner and notorious Euro-hater Harold Ballard. Salming was welcomed into the Hall in 1996.

Most games by a Hall of Famer who played for only one team, career
1,549: Alex Delvecchio, Detroit, 1950–51 to 1973–74
Loyal to the end, Delvecchio skated in 24 NHL seasons, all with Detroit. The streak began on March 25, 1951, when he was called up from junior, and lasted until October 7, 1973, when he retired

to take over as the team's coach. Delvecchio left the game second only to Gordie Howe in games played, assists and points.

Most games by a Hall of Famer who never won a Cup, career
1,432: Mike Gartner, 1979–80 to 1997–98

Gartner played for five teams in his 19-year career, but didn't reach the Stanley Cup finals with any of them. His best shot at getting his name on the silverware was in 1993–94, when he played for the first-place Rangers. New York won the Cup that year, but Gartner wasn't around to enjoy it. He was sent to Toronto at the March trade deadline.

Most games by a Hall of Fame goalie who never won a Cup, career
609: Ed Giacomin, 1965–66 to 1977–78

So near and yet so far. Giacomin starred for some powerful Ranger teams in the early 1970s, but the New Yorkers never made it all the way to the top. Fast Eddie and the Blueshirts came within two wins of getting their hands on Lord Stanley's mug in 1972, only to bow to the Bruins in the finals.

Only Hall of Famer to appear in pro games in six decades
Gordie Howe, 1940s to 1990s

Howe really didn't need to do this. On October 3, 1997, the 69-year-old grandfather signed a one-game contract with the Detroit Vipers of the International Hockey League in order to set a record that no one could topple: the only hockey player to appear in pro games in six decades. Howe started the game at right wing, played one shift of 47 seconds and did not touch the puck. Perhaps the most unsettling image of the entire episode was seeing Mr. Hockey emerge onto the ice through an inflated green snake head that was hissing fog.

First Hall of Famer to voluntarily unretire his number
Milt Schmidt, Boston, 1957

It's strange how some players never develop as predicted. While coaching Boston in 1956–57, Schmidt thought so highly of young winger Larry Regan that he unretired his No. 15 and gave it to the Bruins rookie. The expectations that came with wearing No. 15 proved too heavy for Regan, however, who won the Calder Trophy in 1957 but then faded quickly. Schmidt is not the only Hall of Famer to take his number out of mothballs. In 1972, Ace Bailey, who worked as a gatekeeper at Maple Leaf Gardens, asked Toronto's management to unretire his No. 6 so that winger Ron Ellis could wear it.

First Hall of Famer to have his number involuntarily unretired
Dit Clapper, Boston, 1983

Six years after Clapper's death and contrary to the wishes of the Hall of Famer's family, Bruins GM Harry Sinden opted to unretire Clapper's No. 5 and give it to newly acquired defenseman Guy Lapointe. This was the same Lapointe who had spent the previous 14 years playing with Montreal—Boston's most-loathed rival. Predictably, the move enraged many Bruins fans. Boston hockey writer Leo Monahan called the decision "ghoulish." Lapointe wore No. 5 in 45 games for Boston in 1983–84. After the season, Lapointe retired and Clapper's number was put on ice for a second time.

Only Hall of Famer to overcome two spinal fusions

Rod Gilbert, 1960–61 to 1977–78

Gilbert broke his fifth vertebra when he slipped on an ice-cream wrapper and fell awkwardly into the boards during his last junior game in 1961. Doctors saved his career by performing a spinal fusion, using bone taken from his left leg, though he developed a blood clot in his leg as a result and needed a life-saving operation. Gilbert recovered and went on to become a star winger with the New York Rangers, only to be sidelined again in January 1966, when he had to undergo a second spinal fusion to repair the disintegrating bones in his back. This time, Gilbert "died" on the operating table. As he later recalled: "I was gone for maybe three or four minutes and I left my body. It was an amazing experience. I looked down from above the table and I saw them working on me, trying to restore my heartbeat. Emile Francis was there, and when the nurse said, 'I think we lost him,' Emile jumped up and shouted, 'You can't lose him. He's my best right-winger. Bring him back!' And somehow they brought me back." Gilbert played another 12 years, establishing himself as one of the game's elite snipers. When he retired in 1978, he owned 20 Rangers scoring records and was the second-highest-scoring right-winger in history next to Gordie Howe.

Only Hall of Famer sidelined with polio

Bill Gadsby, 1952

Prior to the 1952–53 season, doctors discovered that Gadsby had polio in 58 per cent of his body (65 per cent would have meant paralysis). But Gadsby took the required medication and made a swift and full recovery, returning to play virtually the entire season. His display of grit and commitment earned him election as Chicago's captain.

Only Hall of Famer suspended for gambling
Babe Pratt, January 29, 1946

Pratt, a star defenseman who scored the Cup-winning goal for the 1945 champion Toronto Maple Leafs, saw his status change from hero to zero almost overnight. Midway through the 1946–47 season, he was expelled from the NHL for "conduct prejudicial to the welfare of hockey." Translation: Pratt bet on NHL games. At his appeal, Pratt admitted to gambling and promised not to do it again. Miraculously, he was reinstated 16 days later by the league after missing only five games. Pratt entered the Hall in 1966.

Only Hall of Famer to have his face on a "Wanted" poster
Eddie Shore, 1926–27 to 1939–40

Shore was public enemy number one at all NHL rinks outside Boston, a player known as much for his toughness as for his skill. During the late 1920s, New York Rangers owner Tex Rickard would publicize Shore and the Bruins' visits to Madison Square Garden by having ambulances race down New York's Theatre Row. Hyped by the promise of a bloodletting, the clashes with the Bruins regularly sold out in New York. Rickard once went so far as to promote a tilt against Boston by using a "Wanted Dead or Alive" poster featuring Shore's picture.

Most penalty minutes by a Hall of Famer, career
1,808: Ted Lindsay, 1944–45 to 1964–65

They did not call Lindsay "Terrible Ted" for nothing. Mayhem and Lindsay were a package deal. The rowdy winger hacked, slashed and fought his way to an NHL-record 1,808 penalty minutes. The mark stood for a decade, until it was broken by Bryan Watson.

Fewest penalty minutes by a Hall of Famer, career (min. 300 games)
24: Clint Smith, 1936–37 to 1946–47

The sin bin was unfamiliar territory for Smith, who never accumulated more than six penalty minutes in any of his 11 seasons and who had three seasons with zero minutes. A winner of the Lady Byng Trophy with the Rangers in 1939 and with the Blackhawks in 1944, Smith recorded 397 points in 483 career games.

Only Hall of Famer to compete in the Summer Olympics
Syl Apps Sr., 1936

An inspirational leader and a superb athlete, Apps excelled at hockey, football and track and field. He held the Canadian record for the pole vault from 1936 until 1948, won a gold medal in the event at the 1934 British Games and competed for Canada at the 1936 Olympics in Berlin, finishing sixth. Apps joined the Toronto Maple Leafs after the Olympics, and in his first season led the NHL in assists and was second in goal scoring, winning the 1937 Calder Trophy as rookie of the year. He later captained the Leafs to three Stanley Cups. In addition to being inducted into the Hockey Hall of Fame, Apps is also a member of the Canadian Sports Hall of Fame and the Canadian Amateur Athlete Hall of Fame.

Only Hall of Famer to change a Hall of Fame rule by boycotting his own induction ceremony
Ted Lindsay, 1966

The Hall waved its mandatory five-year waiting period and inducted Lindsay shortly after his retirement in 1966. But when the winger learned that the banquet was a males-only affair, he wrote a letter of complaint, explaining that his wife had sacrificed a lot to allow him to play in the NHL and that he wanted her to be there to share in the honour. The Hall refused to bend and Lindsay boycotted the ceremony. But he had made his point. The following year, the Hall changed its regulations and admitted women to the gala evening.

Most planes shot down by a Hall of Famer

12: Art Duncan, 1926–27 to 1930–31

Duncan must have been quite a player in his prime. In 1923–24, with Vancouver, he led the Pacific Coast Hockey Association in goals and points—and Duncan was a defenseman! He later played in the NHL with the Detroit Cougars and the Toronto Maple Leafs. Duncan's courage and leadership qualities were proven during World War I, when he served as a fighter pilot with the Royal Flying Corps, downing a dozen enemy aircraft and earning himself the Military Cross.

Most photo-shy Hall of Famer

Frank Brimsek, 1938–39 to 1949–50

Brimsek had a thing about his eyes. The goalie believed they were the keys to his fortune and avoided anything that might possibly damage them, including flashbulbs, which he considered a major threat to his retinas. Any time a photographer got within range, he would cover his peepers with a towel. It was a constant battle because Brimsek was such an irresistible subject. Good-looking, supremely cool and extremely talented, he backstopped the Bruins to the Stanley Cup in his rookie season and went on to register 252 wins and 40 shutouts in a 514-game career.

Shortest player elected to the Hall of Fame
Roy Worters, 1925–26 to 1936–37
Small in size but not in stature, Worters was elected to the
Hall in 1969. Nicknamed "Shrimp" because of his diminutive
five-foot-three, 135-pound frame, the Toronto-born netminder
enjoyed a celebrated 12-year NHL career, winning the Hart
Trophy in 1929 and the Vezina Trophy in 1931 despite playing
for the New York Americans, one of the league's weakest teams.

Most children fathered by a Hall of Famer
22: Georges Vezina, 1917–18 to 1925–26
Birth control was an unknown concept in the Vezina household,
but family tragedy was not. The Montreal Canadiens goalie great
died at age 39 of tuberculosis, and only two of his 22 children
lived to adulthood.

Highest goals-against average by a Hall of Fame goalie, career
3.38: Grant Fuhr, 1981–82 to 1999–2000
Fuhr owns some very atypical stats for a Hall of Fame goalie: 15
seasons with a GAA above 3.00, only 25 shutouts in 868 games
and an unimpressive save percentage of .887.

Only Hall of Fame goalie who never recorded a winning season
Charlie Rayner, 1940–41 to 1952–53
Rayner's career won-lost-tie record was an uninspiring
138–208–77, but he was a far better goalie than the numbers
suggest. His fans knew it; so too did the Hall of Fame selection
committee. But Rayner's curse was that he spent his career in
New York, first with the lowly Americans in the early 1940s, then
with the struggling Rangers during the late 1940s and early
1950s. The only year Rayner came close to a winning season was
in 1949–50, when he had a 28–30–11 record. That season, he won

the Hart Trophy as league MVP and carried the upstart Rangers
to within one win of the Cup.

Most NHL teams played for by a Hall of Famer
9: Paul Coffey, 1980–81 to 2000–01

Coffey, who collected 1,531 career points, is regarded as one of the
greatest offensive defensemen of all time, so it's strange how often
the Hall of Famer switched home addresses. During his 21-year career
he played for nine different teams, six of them in his last six seasons,
when he was passed around like a day-old newspaper. After being
released by Boston in December 2000, Coffey tried for 10 months to
find another team to sign him, but found no takers.

Only Hall of Famer to die as a result of an injury suffered in a game
Howie Morenz, March 8, 1937

There are few people still alive who saw Morenz in his heyday,
but according to eyewitnesses, it was his skating that set him
apart. The Stratford Streak ignited hockey fans like no one else.
The response was most frenzied in Montreal, the site of
Morenz's glory days in the late 1920s and early 1930s. Traded to
Chicago in October 1934, Morenz would be reacquired two years
later by the Canadiens. He returned to a heroic welcome, but
tragedy awaited. On January 28, 1937, in a game against the
Blackhawks, he was checked into the boards and broke his leg, a
career-ending injury. The 34-year-old forward never left the hospital. On March 8, the hockey world was stunned by the news of
his death. The official cause was a heart attack, but the fans
knew better: Morenz had died of a broken heart.

Only Hall of Famer to die after a brawl with a teammate
Terry Sawchuk, May 31, 1970

Sawchuk's star-crossed life came to a bizarre end in 1970, when he and Ranger teammate Ron Stewart got into a drunken backyard brawl over the issue of who was responsible for cleaning up their rental house. In the tussle, Sawchuk fell on a barbecue stake and suffered severe internal injuries. He died a few days later in hospital after complications from intestinal surgery, at age 40. The police initially considered charging Stewart in Sawchuk's death, but later cleared him of any wrongdoing.

Most people to view a Hall of Famer's casket
115,000: Maurice Richard, May 30, 2000

Unlike the modest life Richard tried to live as the reluctant hero of an adoring public, in death his funeral mass at Montreal's Notre Dame Basilica turned into an extravaganza that drew a who's who of Canadian society and hockey. The 90-minute service was attended by 800 invited guests, including prime ministers, hockey legends and other dignitaries. In addition, more than 2,200 fans filled the second- and third-floor balconies, some wearing Montreal Canadiens sweaters, while thousands more watched from outside and hundreds of thousands more viewed the spectacle on national television. The day before the mass, an estimated 115,000 mourners filed silently by Richard's open casket, which was placed between the blueline and the goal at Montreal's Molson Centre.

CHAPTER 4

Unsettling
scores

Todd Bertuzzi's sneak attack on Colorado's Steve Moore on March 8, 2004, ignited a record-setting uproar. Some felt he should be banned for life for giving Moore a concussion and breaking three bones in his neck. Bertuzzi was seeking revenge for a Moore hit that knocked Canucks captain Markus Naslund cold in an earlier game. It wasn't the first time a player has tried to settle a score, with ugly consequences.

Most horrifying injury in a regular-season game

Ace Bailey, Toronto, December 12, 1933

Angry because he had been belted into the boards without a
penalty being called, Boston great Eddie Shore took out his frustration on Toronto's Ace Bailey, blindsiding him from the rear.
Shore's hit sent the right-winger crashing to the ice headfirst in
a pool of blood. Bailey's teammate Red Horner responded by
punching Shore and knocking him cold. Shore's head hit the ice
and he too began bleeding. Shore needed 16 stitches, but Bailey's
condition was more serious—he had a fractured skull. As Bailey
lay near death in hospital, police made preparations to charge
Shore with manslaughter. But surgeons saved Bailey's life with
two delicate operations and he made a miraculous recovery,
though he never played again. Despite Toronto's attempts to
have Shore suspended for the balance of the season, he only
received a 16-game ban—most of which he spent holidaying in
Bermuda.

Most horrifying injury in a preseason game

Ted Green, Boston, September 21, 1969

Green's stick-swinging duel with St. Louis forward Wayne Maki
during a 1969 exhibition match raised the bar in ugly hockey.
Maki's vicious two-hander across Green's skull smashed through
to the player's brain and left the Boston defenseman convulsing
on the ice. Surgeons performed brain surgery, even though they
didn't expect Green to live. He eventually pulled through after
undergoing three major operations and having a steel plate
inserted in his head. Maki was suspended for 30 days and Green
for 12 games when he returned to action a year later. Assault
charges were filed against both players, but both were acquitted.

Most horrifying injury to a goalie
Clint Malarchuk, Buffalo, March 22, 1989

In a goal-crease collision during the 1988–89 season, Malarchuk's jugular was sliced by St. Louis rookie Steve Tuttle's skateblade. TV cameras followed Malarchuk as he raced to the bench gripping his throat while blood spurted through his fingers. The team's trainer and doctors controlled the bleeding, then rushed the stricken goalie to hospital. Amazingly, Malarchuk was back in the Sabres' net 11 days later, 300 stitches the wiser.

Most horrifying injury to a superstar
Gordie Howe, Detroit, March 28, 1950

During an up-ice rush to catch Ted Kennedy during the 1950 semifinals against Toronto, Howe lost his balance and crashed headfirst into the boards. That's the official story, anyway. Many at the game saw Kennedy dump the puck ahead and stop just at the point of collision. Apparently, he then butt-ended Howe in the face, causing him to lose his footing in mid-stride. As Howe fell, Detroit defenseman Black Jack Stewart, who also had Kennedy in his sights, accidentally slammed into Howe from the side. There was no game footage to prove exactly what happened, but photographs shot seconds later show Howe unconscious on the ice, bleeding profusely from the head and face. When smelling salts didn't work, he was strapped to a gurney and rushed to hospital, where doctors repaired Howe's broken nose and cheekbone and cut into his skull to relieve the swelling in his brain. Even without its superstar, however, Detroit captured the Cup. Howe wore a helmet the next season.

Most unsportsmanlike hit after being burned by a giveaway
Dale Hunter, Washington, April 28, 1993

Old-time hockey saw plenty of late hits, but Hunter gets tagged here in consideration of his 1993 21-game suspension—at the time the longest player-on-player infraction in NHL history. Hunter's infamous cheap shot was a blindside check on New York Islanders forward Pierre Turgeon, who had just scored a playoff-series-winning goal after stealing the puck from Hunter. In retaliation, the Washington captain drilled Turgeon while his arms were raised in celebration. Turgeon hit the boards hard and sustained a separated shoulder, eliminating him from the next playoff round. Hunter and the Capitals were each fined US$150,000, and Hunter served his 21-game suspension the next season.

Most knockouts by a superstar, establishing his reputation, one game
2: Maurice Richard, Montreal, December 17, 1944

When Richard stepped onto the NHL scene, coaches threw every obstacle in his path to stop him from scoring, including hiring hit men such as Bob "Killer" Dill. A practised boxer with two famous fighting uncles, Tom and Mike Gibbons, Dill got kicked out of the AHL for assaulting a referee. Those credentials were good enough for New York Rangers coach Frank Boucher, whose lineup of wartime replacements faced certain embarrassment on home ice against the speedy Canadiens in December 1944. By the second period, Madison Square Garden was crackling with the anticipation of a Rocket-Killer bout. Dill taunted Richard with sticks, elbows and insults, but some say it was "goddamn

Canuck" or "cowardly frog" that finally did it, something the unilingual Richard would understand. After trading punches, Richard landed a powerful right to Dill's jaw that dropped the defenseman. When the fog lifted and with both men in the penalty box, Dill had another go at Richard, who was just feet away without any barrier between the two of them. A flurry of fists, and Dill took another shot that knocked him out. If Richard was going to make his mark, he picked the right town: New York, where they knew their fights. Some scribes called Richard the best one-two puncher to come along since Joe Louis. The next time the Canadiens visited MSG, more than 15,000 fans jammed the arena.

Only player suspended for assaulting a fan with his own shoe

Mike Milbury, Boston, December 23, 1979

The trouble started at the end of a 1979 Bruins-Rangers game, when Ranger goalie John Davidson accused Boston's Al Secord of sucker-punching Ranger Ulf Nilsson. The argument escalated as a cluster of players drifted toward the Boston exit corner, at which point the Bruins realized that Stan Jonathan had been struck and cut under the eye with a thrown object and Terry O'Reilly was being menaced by a stick-wielding fan. Several Boston players scaled the boards and fought with the spectators, including O'Reilly, Secord, Peter McNab and Mike Milbury, who removed one fan's shoe and beat the man with it. After 10 minutes of wild scuffling, Garden security finally separated the players and spectators. The Bruins retreated to their dressing room in a hail of garbage as police struggled to keep fans from reaching the ice. Milbury received a two-game suspension for his unorthodox assault.

First player indicted by a grand jury for aggravated assault with a deadly weapon (a stick)

Dave Forbes, Boston, 1975

Henry Boucha of the Minnesota North Stars and Dave Forbes of the Boston Bruins tangled twice in a game on January 4, 1975, with tragic results. While leaving the penalty box after their first altercation, Forbes jabbed Boucha with the butt end of his stick, cutting him above the eye and knocking him down. Forbes then began raining punches on the fallen North Star. After peace was restored, Boucha was carried off on a stretcher. The cut required 30 stitches to close, but, more seriously, Boucha's right eye-socket had been fractured. Despite surgery, his sight never returned to normal and he soon retired. Forbes was indicted by a grand jury in Minnesota for aggravated assault with a deadly weapon and brought to trial. The case ended in a hung jury. In 1976, Boucha filed a us$3.5-million damage suit against Forbes and the NHL. Four years later, he received an out-of-court settlement of us$1.5 million, the largest payment ever awarded for an injury sustained during an NHL game.

First NHL player to file a civil suit for an on-ice injury

Denis Polonich, Detroit, 1978

Polonich was sidelined with a broken nose and severe facial injuries after he was clobbered by Colorado's Wilf Paiement during a stick-swinging fight on October 25, 1978. Paiement, who was given a match penalty, was retaliating for a cross-check in the face that he had received from Polonich. The incident led to a 15-game suspension for Paiement and a civil lawsuit against Paiement and Colorado, which Polonich won on August 17, 1982. The Red Wing was awarded us$850,000 in damages.

First former NHL player convicted of manslaughter
Tony Demers, 1949

Demers, who played six NHL seasons for the Montreal Canadiens and the New York Rangers in the early 1940s, had just posted a 111-point season with Sherbrooke of the Quebec Senior League and been voted the most gentlemanly player in the league. But his world changed on the night of September 15, 1949, when he got into a drunken argument with his girlfriend and beat her to death. Demers claimed that she had sustained her injuries by jumping from his moving car. Regardless, he did not take the unconscious woman to hospital until the next morning. Demers was initially charged with murder, but the jury recommended the charge be reduced to manslaughter. He was convicted and sentenced to 15 years.

First NHL player charged with arranging a murder
Mike Danton, St. Louis, April 16, 2004

Bizarre doesn't quite cover it. At the same time as his team was being eliminated from the playoffs, the Blues forward was trying to eliminate another human being. In April 2004, Danton was charged by the FBI for his role in a murder-for-hire plot. According to news reports, Danton asked a 19-year-old friend named Katie Wolfmeyer if she could find someone to perform a murder for US$10,000. The individual Wolfmeyer contacted then went to the police. Danton supposedly told her that the target was a hit man who was coming from Canada to kill him, but the FBI report stated that Danton was actually trying to kill his agent, David Frost, who had threatened to go to St. Louis management and ruin his career after a quarrel about Danton's "promiscuity and use of alcohol." (As we went to press, this messy saga was still unravelling.)

First player sentenced to jail time for an on-ice attack

Dino Ciccarelli, Minnesota, 1988

The NHL suspended Ciccarelli—Minnesota's leading scorer—10 games for twice whacking Toronto defenseman Luke Richardson over the head with his stick during a game on January 6, 1988, at Maple Leaf Gardens. Richardson was not injured, but after receiving complaints from fans, Toronto authorities charged Ciccarelli with assault. Later that summer, the player went on trial and was convicted and sentenced to one day in jail. Ciccarelli was fingerprinted and photographed in the city hoosegow, but did not spend the night in a cell. It was the first and only time that an NHL player has been sent to jail for an on-ice offense, establishing a sentencing precedent that remained in place until Marty McSorley's conviction 12 years later.

First player suspended for games against one team

Bernie Geoffrion, Montreal, 1953–54

Furious after being speared by Ranger Ron Murphy, Geoffrion swung his stick like a baseball bat and caught Murphy flush in the face. The winger suffered a fractured jaw and a concussion. NHL president Clarence Campbell gave Murphy a five-game suspension, but he got more creative with Geoffrion's punishment. To avoid possible retaliation, Campbell suspended Geoffrion for the remaining eight regular-season games between the Rangers and the Canadiens.

First player banned from playing in another city

Dan Maloney, Detroit, 1975–76

On November 5, 1975, Maloney jumped Brian Glennie from behind after the Toronto Maple Leaf defenseman flattened

Detroit's Bryan Hextall Jr. with a bodycheck. Maloney rode Glennie to the Maple Leaf Gardens ice, then picked him up by the jersey and repeatedly smashed him face-first into the ice. Glennie was taken to hospital with a concussion and missed two games. Police charged Maloney with assault causing bodily harm the next day. Charges were dropped when Maloney agreed to plead no contest and perform community service work. As part of his unique sentence, the Detroit enforcer was also banned from playing in Toronto for two years. The Leafs must have been impressed. After Maloney's exile ended, he was acquired by Toronto in a trade and later coached the Leafs.

First player suspended for instigating a brawl before a game
Ed Hospodar, Philadelphia, May 14, 1987

A ritual that Shayne Corson and Claude Lemieux developed, of shooting the puck into the opponent's net at the end of the pregame skate, sparked a donnybrook prior to Game 6 of the 1987 Wales Conference finals between Montreal and Philadelphia. On that night, Flyers tough guy Ed Hopsodar and backup netminder Chico Resch decided to put a stop to the ritual. They stayed on the ice, guarding their net, until Lemieux and Corson left. Hospodar and Resch then retreated to their bench, just in time to see the two Habs pop back on the ice and race toward the Philly net. Resch threw his stick at the puck, but to no avail. Hospodar charged after Lemieux and began pounding the Montreal winger. Within moments, players from both teams in various stages of undress had raced back on the ice and were tossing punches. Since there were no officials on the ice, the battle raged unimpeded for 10 minutes. Hospodar was suspended for the rest of the playoffs for being the instigator of the affair, and the two clubs were assessed US$25,000 in fines.

Only NHL player fined for writing a magazine article about hockey violence

Andy Bathgate, NY Rangers, December 21, 1959

In 1959, Bathgate authored an article in *True* magazine entitled "Atrocities on Ice," in which the Rangers star complained about the level of violence in the NHL, especially the tactic of spearing, stating that if nothing was done about it then "someone is going to get killed." Bathgate named six "spearing specialists": Montreal's Doug Harvey and Tom Johnson; Boston's Fern Flaman; Chicago's Ted Lindsay and Pierre Pilote; and Lou Fontinato from Bathgate's own team. He then stated: "None of them seems to care that he'll be branded as a hockey killer." (In fact, Harvey almost killed Ranger Red Sullivan, when he ruptured his spleen with a vicious spear in a game on November 25, 1956.) Bathgate also called Gordie Howe the "meanest player in the game." NHL president Clarence Campbell fined Bathgate $500 (his fee for the story), claiming that his comments were "prejudicial to the league and the game."

Longest suspension of a player who later became an NHL coach

15 games: Tony Granato, Los Angeles, 1994

Before he was hired as coach of the Colorado Avalanche, Granato had a reputation as a hothead. In a game on February 9, 1994, between the Kings and Blackhawks, he lost his cool after being flattened by Neil Wilkinson with a hard but clean check. After getting to his skates, Granato unloaded a two-handed tomahawk chop to Wilkinson's helmet that left the Chicago defenseman lying on the ice like a broken doll. Granato was suspended for 15 games.

Most fights by a future referee in his first NHL game as a player
Paul Stewart, Quebec, November 22, 1979

The Quebec Nordiques called the pugnacious Stewart up from the minors because they feared that the Boston Bruins would seek vengeance on Robbie Ftorek, who had high-sticked Bobby Schmautz in the two clubs' last meeting. The Boston-born Stewart had a memorable debut. He fought the Bruins' three toughest players—Terry O'Reilly, Stan Jonathan and Al Secord—in the first period before being ejected with a game misconduct. As Stewart passed a TV camera on his way off the ice, he stopped and bowed. Stewart's career lasted only 21 games. Seven years after retiring, he returned to the NHL as a referee.

Most cross-checks by an NHLer that eliminated superstars from international competition
2: Gary Suter, on Wayne Gretzky (1991) and Paul Kariya (1998)

Suter specialized in cheap shots. During the 1991 Canada Cup, the American-born defenseman drilled Team Canada's Wayne Gretzky into the boards from behind with a cross-check, injuring his back. Gretzky missed the rest of the tournament, and his back was never the same. On February 1, 1998, Suter smashed Anaheim's Paul Kariya in the face with a cross-check as Kariya was celebrating a goal against Suter's Blackhawks. Although Kariya never lost consciousness, he suffered a serious head injury and later began experiencing severe headaches, nausea and memory loss. Suter was suspended for just four games, while Kariya, with post-concussion syndrome, missed the final 28 games of the season plus his chance to play in the 1998 Olympics.

Most hockey sticks used in an assault on another player

3: Maurice Richard, Montreal, March 13, 1955

They say that nothing ignited Richard's temper more than the sight of his own blood. In this case, a high stick from Boston's Hal Laycoe drew claret, sending him into a fury. Richard immediately set after the bespectacled Bruins defenseman and slashed him across the shoulders with his stick. The linesmen jumped in and grabbed Richard's stick and separated the two players, but the Rocket broke away, grabbed another stick and slashed Laycoe again. Again the linesmen intervened and again Richard broke loose, found another stick and clubbed Laycoe a third time. Linesman Cliff Thompson then tackled the Rocket from behind, but with the help of a teammate, Richard got free and lashed out at Thompson, firing a couple of hard jabs into his face. As punishment, Richard was suspended for the last three games of the season and the playoffs. Minus their top scorer, the Canadiens lost the finals to Detroit in seven games.

Most automatic suspensions, one game

3: Gordie Dwyer, Tampa Bay, September 19, 2000

During a preseason game against the Washington Capitals, Dwyer left the penalty box to get at Washington's Joe Reekie, with whom he had scuffled earlier. In the scrum that followed, Dwyer bumped linesman David Brisebois and dragged referee Mark Faucette to the ice. Dwyer was assessed three automatic suspensions—totalling 23 games—for his actions: 10 games for physical abuse of officials, 10 games for leaving the penalty box and three games for three game-misconduct penalties. Dwyer later claimed that he didn't remember what set him off. "I don't know. I just lost my temper. I got excited. For sure, I wasn't thinking about the consequences, and didn't understand the consequences, either."

First player to break an opponent's jaw with a sucker punch

Jimmy Mann, Winnipeg, January 13, 1982

Mann shattered Paul Gardner's jaw in two places with a sucker punch, causing the Pittsburgh Penguin sniper to miss 21 games. Mann had left the bench to join a brawl and cold-cocked Gardner as he was talking to a linesman. Mann told the *Globe and Mail* that the punch was in response to an earlier Gardner cross-check to the face of teammate Doug Smail. "Smail was just coming off a broken jaw. I saw Gardner and it looked to me like he was laughing. I said, 'You son of a bitch' and I suckered him." The province of Manitoba charged Mann and gave him a $500 fine for a summary conviction for assault but no jail time. The NHL suspended him for 10 games.

First player to end another player's career with a sucker punch

Matt Johnson, Los Angeles, November 19, 1998

Reportedly angered by a slew-foot delivered by Jeff Beukeboom to teammate Glen Murray, Johnson challenged Beukeboom to a fight. When the Ranger declined to drop his gloves, Johnson socked him in the back of the head. Beukeboom collapsed to the ice face-first and was still wobbly when he left the ice with help from medical personnel a few minutes later. Johnson received a 12-game suspension. Beukeboom returned to play briefly later that season, but immediately suffered two more concussions—the last one after a seemingly harmless bump from Carolina forward Martin Gelinas—and was forced to retire.

Most popular sucker punch

Tie Domi on Ulf Samuelsson, October 14, 1995

For much of his career, Samuelsson was the most hated player in hockey, widely regarded as a sneaky, low-down coward. So in 1995, when Domi dropped the Swedish defenseman with an unexpected left to the jaw with 64 seconds left in a 2–0 Rangers victory in Toronto, many cheered. Samuelsson's head bounced twice on the ice and he lay flat for five minutes before being helped off. He took four stitches to the back of his head and suffered a concussion. Domi was fined US$1,000, the maximum allowed by the terms of the NHLPA collective bargaining agreement, and was suspended for eight games. Although the punch seemed to come out of nowhere, Domi claimed he was hoping for a fair fight. "I didn't know he wasn't going to drop his gloves," he said. "I'm sure not known for my sucker punches."

Most premeditated surprise hit
Tie Domi on Scott Niedermayer, May 3, 2001

Domi levelled Scott Niedermayer with a surprise elbow to the head in the waning moments of Game 4 of the 2001 Eastern Conference semifinals as the two players skated by one another behind the play. The Devils defenseman was briefly knocked unconscious. Afterward, Niedermayer claimed Domi had threatened to hit him two games before in retaliation for getting clipped for a cut over the nose, and had even boasted it would be bad enough for a suspension. Domi got his wish—he was banned for 11 games. The Maple Leafs tough guy said he regretted what had happened, calling it a "stupid reaction."

Largest loss of salary for a sucker punch

US$501,000: Todd Bertuzzi, Vancouver, March 2004

When Bertuzzi sucker-punched Steve Moore from behind and
drove the unconscious Colorado forward's face into the ice, he
also gave hockey a black eye. Moore went to hospital with a concussion, facial cuts and three broken bones in his neck, while
Bertuzzi was suspended for the rest of the season and the playoffs. Yet despite the huge public outcry, the NHL did not fine
Bertuzzi for his attack. However, he was forced to forfeit
US$501,926.23, the amount he would have earned for the
final 13 games of the regular season, which was turned over
to the NHL Players' Emergency Fund. The Canucks were also
fined US$250,000, for their responsibility in the incident. In
response to media criticism, Canucks general manager Brian
Burke defended Bertuzzi, calling him a "great hockey player
and warm human being," and also insisted that the team's fine
and any suggestion that coach Marc Crawford was at fault was
"horribly unjust."

First GM suspended for sucker-punching a coach

George McPhee, Washington, 1999

McPhee blew a fuse following a preseason game on September
25, 1999. Upset by the violent tactics employed by the Chicago
Blackhawks, the Capitals' GM stormed into the Chicago locker
room and began pummelling Blackhawks coach Lorne
Molleken. Several Blackhawks players and arena security guards
jumped in to stop the fracas, but not before McPhee had black-
ened one of Molleken's eyes. McPhee himself was bleeding from
the face and missing an entire arm of his suit jacket. But at least
he'd made his point: violence has no place in hockey. The NHL hit
McPhee with a month-long suspension and a US$20,000 fine.

First player suspended for an entire calendar year

Marty McSorley, Boston, February 23, 2000

Frustrated after losing a fight to Vancouver's Donald Brashear, McSorley tracked down the Canuck winger in the final minute and hacked him on the side of the head with his stick. Brashear was knocked unconscious when his head hit the ice. A B.C. provincial court later found McSorley guilty of assault with a weapon, but gave him a conditional discharge. He was also suspended for the last 23 games of the season and the playoffs, and NHL commissioner Gary Bettman later extended the sentence to a full calendar year. When McSorley's ban ended, no NHL team would offer him a contract.

Most violent reaction to a *Hockey Night in Canada* telecast

Roy Spencer, December 12, 1970

We can understand Spencer being upset, but not his reaction. When CBC affiliates in British Columbia chose to broadcast a game between Vancouver and California instead of an Original Six game between Toronto and Chicago, in which Spencer's son Brian was making his TV debut with the Leafs, Spencer senior drove two hours to a Prince George TV station. Upon arriving, he pulled out a pistol, took the employees hostage and cut the station's power. When the RCMP showed up, Spencer became embroiled in a shootout and was killed. Brian Spencer was told about his father's death after the Leafs-Chicago game. He stubbornly played in Toronto's next game, a 4–0 win over Buffalo in which he picked up three assists. Guns and misfortune were endemic in the Spencer family. In 1998, Brian Spencer was shot and killed in Florida during a drug deal.

CHAPTER 5

Turning
tricks

Gordie Howe scored more career

goals than Maurice Richard, but the

Rocket had more hat tricks—27 to 19. Yet, unlike

Howe, Richard never had a hat trick named after

him. A player completes a "Gordie Howe hat trick"

when he scores a goal and an assist and gets into a

fight. In this chapter, we salute the hat trick and

other unusual scoring feats.

Most hat tricks, career

50: Wayne Gretzky, 1979–80 to 1998–99
40: Mario Lemieux, 1984–85 to 2003–04

The king of the tricksters got his 50th against Vancouver on October 11, 1997. The Rangers were in town to play their first game against former captain Mark Messier, who had left the team to sign with the Canucks prior to the season. But Gretzky had another incentive to play well—he was still upset about the way Vancouver's management had accused him of negotiating in bad faith a year earlier when the Canucks had made an unsuccessful attempt to sign him. Gretzky vented his anger on the home team, netting three goals and setting up two more in a 6–3 Rangers victory. Gretzky's third goal, a mesmerizing effort that left a trail of hapless defenders sprawled on the ice, drew thunderous applause from the Vancouver crowd.

Most hat tricks by a defenseman, career

9: Bobby Orr, 1966–67 to 1978–79

How common is it for defensemen to score hat tricks? Not very. Ray Bourque, the NHL's all-time leading scorer among blueliners, registered only one in his 21-year career. Paul Coffey, second in scoring by a defenseman, totalled four. Orr had nine.

Most hat tricks, one season

10: Wayne Gretzky, Edmonton, 1981–82
10: Wayne Gretzky, Edmonton, 1983–84
9: Mike Bossy, NY Islanders, 1980–81
9: Mario Lemieux, Pittsburgh, 1988–89

It's amazing how many scoring records have Gretzky's finger-prints all over them. No. 99 was a perfect 10 in hat tricks twice with the Edmonton Oilers, the first of which, in 1981–82, erased the mark set the previous year by the Islanders' Mike Bossy.

Most hat tricks by a defenseman, one season
4: Bobby Orr, Boston, 1974–75

Orr scored 46 times in 1974–75, when he pushed the offensive envelope to new dimensions. Boston's golden boy picked on the poor, registering two hat tricks against Washington and one each against Pittsburgh and California.

Most hat tricks in season openers
2: Cam Neely, Boston, January 22, 1995 and October 2, 1995
2: Brendan Shanahan, St. Louis, October 5, 1993 and Detroit, October 4, 2001

Neely notched his pair of tricks in consecutive season openers. The first was in 1994–95's lockout-shortened season against the Flyers; the second was in 1995, versus the Islanders. Shanahan bagged his pair eight years apart. His first came in 1993, against Dallas. He completed his second when he scored a shorthanded goal in overtime against San Jose in 2001.

Most teams played for before recording a hat trick
10: Mike Sillinger, April 11, 2004

It was a long time coming. When the St. Louis Blues picked up Sillinger from Phoenix late in 2003–04, it marked the 10th city in his nomadic 14-year NHL career, tying the record held by Michel Petit and J.J. Daigneault. St. Louis acquired Sillinger as a third-line centre, but he supplied some unsuspected offensive pop down the stretch. His best moment came in Game 3 of the Blues' playoff series with San Jose, when he bagged the first hat trick of his career in a 4–1 Blues win, putting his third goal into an empty net with 45 seconds to go.

First player to record consecutive hat tricks, one game
Darryl Sittler, Toronto, February 7, 1976

Sittler caught lightning in a bottle. Not only did the Maple Leafs captain register an NHL-record 10 points on six goals and four assists in an 11–4 mauling of the Boston Bruins, he also notched hat tricks in both the second and third periods. No other NHLer has ever scored hat tricks in two consecutive periods. Sittler's sixth goal typified his seeing-eye luck: his attempted pass out from behind the Boston cage struck the skates of two Bruins and bounced into the net. "It was a night when every time I had the puck, something seemed to happen," said Sittler afterward. "In other games, you work just as hard and come up empty."

Only player to record a hat trick in overtime
Ken Doraty, Toronto, January 16, 1934

An oddity for sure. Doraty, who scored only 15 career goals, connected at 0:45, 1:35 and 6:45 of overtime for Toronto in a 7–4 win over the Ottawa Senators. It occurred during an era in which overtimes lasted a full 10 minutes, regardless of how many goals were scored.

Fastest hat trick
21 seconds: Bill Mosienko, Chicago, March 23, 1952

It was the last game of the 1951–52 season and the New York Rangers were in command, leading Chicago 6–2 early in the third period. That's when Chicago's top line of Gus Bodnar at centre, George Gee at left wing and Bill Mosienko at right wing took over. Bodnar won the draw to Mosienko, who zipped around Rangers defenseman Hy Buller to snap a low-wrister past rookie goalie Lorne Anderson (time of the goal was 6:09).

The line stayed on the ice for the centre-ice faceoff. Bodnar won the draw straight to Mosienko, who blew past Buller again to fire a shot past Anderson (time of the goal was 6:20). Chicago coach Ebbie Goodfellow decided to stick with his hot line, and again Bodnar won the faceoff. This time, the puck went to Gee, who dashed down the ice and passed to Mosienko, who deked to his left and buried his third goal past Anderson (time of the goal was 6:30). Just 21 seconds, that's all it took. The demoralized Rangers lost 7–6.

Fastest hat trick on one power play

44 seconds: Jean Béliveau, Montreal, November 5, 1955
Up until the 1956–57 season, penalized players had to serve the full duration of their infractions—whether or not the opposition scored on the power play. This meant an efficient power play could inflict severe damage, as was demonstrated in this 1955 game between Boston and Montreal. Boston was up 2–0 in the second period when it made the fatal error of taking two minor penalties. During the ensuing two-man advantage, Béliveau erupted for three goals against goalie Terry Sawchuk. After Béliveau scored his third, Montreal fans littered the Forum ice with hats and programs. And when Béliveau notched his fourth goal of the night to seal a 4-2 victory, the fans rained down another shower of debris.

Fastest hat trick by a defenseman

3:21: Denis Potvin, NY Islanders, October 14, 1978
Potvin was unfairly billed as the "next Bobby Orr" when he joined the Islanders in 1974. Still, a great blueliner in his own right, Potvin scored three straight goals in just over three minutes in the second period of a 1978 game against Toronto. Yet despite his record-breaking contribution, the Islanders lost 10–7.

Fastest hat trick by a rookie

1:52: Carl Liscombe, Detroit, March 13, 1938

Liscombe lit up Chicago goalie Mike Karakas for a trio of first-period goals in a 1:52 span during a 5–1 Detroit win. The outburst set not just a rookie record, but also a new NHL standard, eclipsing the mark set by the Canadiens' Pit Lepine, who pumped in three goals in 2:57 in a 7–1 trampling of the Blackhawks on March 3, 1927.

Fewest shots on net by a player who recorded a hat trick

0: Wayne Dillon, NY Rangers, December 8, 1976

Dillon counted the freakiest hat trick in NHL history in a 4–4 tie with St. Louis. The Rangers centre scored his first goal when his pass deflected off Blues forward Claude Larose and under goalie Ed Johnston. He got credit for his second when defenseman Rod Seiling accidentally knocked the puck into his own net. Dillon completed the hat trick when his errant pass ricocheted into the Blues' net off the skate of defenseman Bruce Affleck. After the game, Johnston remarked: "We scored seven goals tonight and still didn't win."

Age of youngest player to record a hat trick

18.8 years: Jack Hamilton, Toronto, February 19, 1944

Hamilton earned little recognition for his brief 102-game NHL stint. A wartime replacement for the Leafs, he scored only 28 goals before drifting back to the AHL—but this gem has brought new fame to his game. Hamilton was 18 years and 262 days old when he became the NHL's youngest trickster, in Toronto's 10–4 win against Boston.

Age of oldest player to record a hat trick

40.8 years: Gordie Howe, Detroit, November 2, 1969

Howe was 40 years and eight months old when he put three pucks behind Penguins goalie Al Smith in a 4–3 Detroit win. It was Mr. Hockey's 19th and final NHL hat trick. He scored the goals in succession, a pure hat trick.

Age of oldest defenseman to record a hat trick

38.0 years: Dit Clapper, Boston, February 17, 1945

Clapper had just turned 38 when the blueliner accounted for three Boston goals in a 6–1 win over the Rangers. What makes this feat doubly unusual was that Clapper also set the record for the longest time between hat tricks. The last time he had scored three goals in a game was on March 9, 1933, when he was playing right wing, 12 years earlier.

Longest span between first and last hat tricks

19.8 years: Gordie Howe, March 19, 1950 to November 2, 1969

This record offers insight into Howe's incredible longevity. He was still pulling tricks out of his hat two decades after he scored his first one.

Fastest four goals by a player

4:12: Peter Bondra, Washington, February 5, 1994

In 1994, the Slovakian speed merchant provided a stunning show of just how explosive he can be, when he burned the Tampa Bay Lightning for five goals, four of them in 4:12, to set a new league record. Three of the goals came on breakaways or partial breakaways, plays in which Bondra simply blew past opponents to pounce on loose pucks.

Most five-goal games, career
4: Joe Malone, 1917–18 to 1923–24
4: Wayne Gretzky, 1979–80 to 1998–99
Gretzky had quite a few more chances than Malone to run up the score. No. 99's career lasted 1,487 games; Malone only played 126. Malone's total included six- and seven-goal games.

Fewest career goals by a player who recorded a five-goal game
ALL-TIME RECORD
14: Harry Hyland, 1917–18
The right-winger's career was winding down when he joined the NHL, but Hyland still had enough gas left in the tank to score five times against Toronto on December 19, 1917, the NHL's opening night. He scored 14 goals in 17 games—split between the Montreal Wanderers and the Ottawa Senators—that season.

MODERN-DAY RECORD
83: Howie Meeker, 1946–47 to 1953–54
A bad back ended Meeker's career with the Toronto Maple Leafs after eight years, but nothing he ever did in the NHL compared to his magical rookie campaign, when he scored five times in a game against Chicago and won the Calder Trophy—attracting even more votes than a kid named Gordie Howe.

Most goals by a defenseman, one game
5: Ian Turnbull, Toronto, February 2, 1977
Turnbull's five-goal explosion came out of the blue. The Maple Leaf rearguard hadn't scored a goal in his previous 30 games, but magic touched him on February 2, 1977, when he potted two in the second period and three in the third in a 9–1 rout of Detroit. After getting his fourth of the game midway through the final

period, Turnbull then set his sights on the record. His fifth goal, scored at 18:30 of the third, came on a planned play. Borje Salming hit his streaking defense partner with a long pass that set him in on a clear breakaway. Turnbull coolly beat goalie Jim Rutherford and bagged the record.

Only player to be denied a fifth goal on a penalty shot
Sergei Fedorov, Detroit, February 12, 1995
The flashy Fedorov had beaten Los Angeles Kings goalie Kelly Hrudey four times in regulation time: twice at even strength, once on the power play and once shorthanded. When the 4–4 game went to overtime, Fedorov had a chance to score five goals in four different ways. He was awarded a penalty shot at 3:52 of OT, but Hrudey came up big and made the save to avoid complete humiliation.

Most goals in consecutive games
9: Wayne Gretzky, Edmonton, December 27 and 30, 1981
Driven by the desire to be the fastest 50-goal scorer in NHL annals, Gretzky poured it on, scoring four goals in a 10–3 demolition of Los Angeles to notch 45 goals in 38 games. Three nights later, the Great One scored five against Philadelphia to reach the 50-goal mark in 39 games. The two-game scoring rampage also earned Gretzky a lesser-known record: most goals by a player in consecutive games.

Most goals, one road game
6: Red Berenson, St. Louis, November 7, 1968
Smooth-skating Red Berenson turned on the red light six times, the most goals in NHL history by a visiting player, as the Blues stomped the Flyers 8–0. The performance earned the Red Baron a *Sports Illustrated* cover shot.

Most goals by a player with a day job, one game
6: Syd Howe, Detroit, February 3, 1944

Howe slammed six pucks past New York Rangers goalie Ken McAuley as the Red Wings waltzed to a 12–2 triumph. "I wonder what the boys in the shop will say now?" Howe said after the game. Like many US-based NHLers during World War II, Howe had a day job—working at a war plant.

Most unlikely player to score seven consecutive goals
Brian Noonan, Chicago, 1991–92

Noonan, a classic grinder who never once reached the 20-goal mark in 12 NHL seasons, briefly morphed into a superhero for the Blackhawks in December 1991. Getting some unaccustomed time on the power play, he scored seven straight goals in back-to-back games: a 3–3 tie against Winnipeg and a 6–4 loss to Detroit. After this startling display, Chicago coach Mike Keenan declared that Noonan was merely living up to the potential that the team knew he had. Sure, Mike.

Age of youngest player to score on a penalty shot
18.7 years: Nathan Horton, Florida, January 8, 2004

The Panthers rookie broke a 60-year-old NHL record by scoring a penalty-shot goal on Flyers goalie Jeff Hackett—at the age of 18 years, 224 days. Toronto's Jack Hamilton was 38 days older than Horton when he set the mark in 1944.

Only player to score twice on the same penalty shot
Jack Hamilton, Toronto, February 19, 1944

During the 1930s and 1940s, the NHL changed its rules regarding penalty shots so often that even the referees became confused. A classic example occurred during a 1944 game between Boston and Toronto in which Leafs rookie Jack Hamilton was awarded a penalty shot after being hauled down by Bruins captain Dit Clapper. Referee Norm Lamport placed the puck at centre ice, and Hamilton went in and fired a shot past goalie Bert Gardiner. But Boston protested, arguing that the puck should have been set at the Bruins' blueline. Lamport admitted his error, then forced Hamilton to retake the shot from the new start position. The rookie skated in, deked Gardiner and lifted the puck home, becoming the only player to score twice on the "same" penalty shot. This was only one of several oddities connected with the play, however. Hamilton was 18, which made him, at the time, the youngest player to score a goal on a penalty shot. The goal was also his third of the night, making him the youngest NHLer to notch a hat trick.

Shortest span between successful penalty shots
8 days: Milan Hejduk, Colorado, January 11 and 20, 2004
Hejduk had to wait six seasons for a penalty shot, but he made up for lost time by scoring on his first two opportunities. The Czech winger scored his second goal of the game on a penalty shot 59 seconds into overtime, giving the Colorado Avalanche a 5–4 win over Tampa Bay on January 20, 2004. With his game winner, Hejduk set a record for the fewest days between successful penalty shots, scoring his first on January 11 against Chicago. The previous record was held by Woody Dumart, who notched penalty-shot goals 20 days apart for Boston in 1939–40.

Most penalty shots by a player in the first week of his career
2: Esa Pirnes, Los Angeles, 2003–04
Penalty shots are rare—at least for most players. Pirnes is one of only three NHLers awarded penalty shots in back-to-back games.

Toronto's Mike Walton in March 1968 and Buffalo's Brent Peterson in January 1984 are the other two. But Pirnes's penalty shots were awarded in the second and third games of his career. The first was on October 10, 2003, against Pittsburgh's Marc-Andre Fleury; the second was on October 12 against Chicago's Jocelyn Thibault. The Kings' centre was thwarted both times.

Most empty-net goals, career
55: Wayne Gretzky, 1979–80 to 1998–99
No one ever accused Gretzky of being a defensive stud, but he still saw a lot of ice time when his team was protecting leads. Otherwise, he doesn't score 55 empty netters.

First player to score an empty-net goal
Cecil Dillon, NY Rangers, January 12, 1932
During the 1931 playoffs, Art Ross became the first bench boss to pull his goalie for an extra attacker. The next season, the Boston Bruins coach became the first to employ the move during the regular season when he pulled goalie Tiny Thompson, with his club trailing the Rangers 4–3 in the waning seconds of the 10-minute overtime. The strategy failed. Right-winger Cecil Dillon, who had scored New York's go-ahead goal, skated through the entire Bruins team and put the puck into the empty net, capping a 5–3 victory and earning himself a place in history.

CHAPTER 6

Cold
cash

When staging a contract holdout in

1997–98, Sergei Fedorov said: "It's

not about the money, it's about what I believe in."

But after sitting out 59 games, Fedorov agreed to a

six-year deal with Detroit for a tidy $38 million.*

Fourteen million was paid in the form of a signing

bonus, instantly elevating the Russian to the ranks

of the filthy rich. We guess that what Fedorov

believed in was, cash up front.

In this chapter, all figures are in US dollars, unless otherwise noted.

First player to sign a Cdn$100,000 contract

Jean Béliveau, Montreal, October 3, 1953

At a time when most NHLers made less than Cdn$10,000 a year, Béliveau inked a deal with Montreal in 1953 that was worth Cdn$105,000 over five years. It was an astronomical sum at the time, especially for a 22-year-old with only five games of NHL experience.

First superstar traded because of a salary cap

Howie Morenz, Montreal, 1934–35

Squeezed by hard times, the NHL lowered its salary cap to Cdn$62,500 per team and a maximum Cdn$7,000 per player in 1934–35. Dwindling cash reserves caused several teams to cut costs. As part of its economic overhaul, Montreal also traded Howie Morenz, one of hockey's biggest names, to the Blackhawks. Although still a fan favourite, the 31-year-old Morenz was a spent force. He scored only eight goals with Chicago in 1934–35.

Cheapest purchase of a modern-day superstar

Cdn$850,000: Wayne Gretzky, Edmonton, 1978

The foundation of the Edmonton Oilers dynasty was built on this one business transaction. In 1978, after just eight games and six points as an Indianapolis Racer, 17-year-old rookie Wayne Gretzky was sold to the Oilers for Cdn$850,000 by Racers owner Nelson Skalbania. Skalbania had originally signed Gretzky to a personal-services contract, but, after losing $40,000 per game in Indianapolis, he was forced to sever ties with the teenager.

Cheapest price paid for a future 50-goal scorer

$1: Ray Sheppard, July 9, 1990

Buffalo thought so little of the slow-footed Sheppard that they sold him to the Rangers for $1 and future considerations after the 1989–90 season. Sheppard scored 24 goals in 59 games for the Rangers in 1990–91, but the Blueshirts still found him wanting. They released him, and he signed as a free agent with the Red Wings. In 1993–94, he rang up 52 goals for Detroit.

Largest single-season increase in salary

$13.9 million: Joe Sakic, Colorado, 1997–98
$9 million: Chris Gratton, Philadelphia, 1997–98

Sakic and Gratton cashed in as free agents when rival teams bid for their services by writing exorbitant offer sheets. Colorado bit the bullet and denied the Rangers by signing Sakic; Tampa Bay wisely let Gratton go to Philadelphia.

Largest single-season percentage increase in salary

981%: Alexander Mogilny, Buffalo, 1993–94
971%: Martin Brodeur, New Jersey, 1995–96

By NHL standards, Mogilny and Brodeur were both badly underpaid on their first contracts. Mogilny, a 76-goal scorer, made $185,000 a year in 1992–93. Brodeur, who led New Jersey to the Cup in 1994–95, was earning a mere $140,000. But both got large raises when they signed new deals. Mogilny's salary increased to $3 million a year, while Brodeur's was bumped up to $1.5 million.

Most honest assessment of the size of NHL salaries by a player

Brett Hull, Detroit, 2003

Asked by the *Hockey News* in December 2003 for his opinion on skyrocketing player salaries, Hull replied: "Bob Goodenow (NHLPA president) will kill me, but if we're going to be realistic about things, probably 75 per cent of the league is overpaid." Presumably, Hull, who was making $5 million a year, included himself in that category.

Most money refused by a player
$3 million: Dominik Hasek, 2003–04

Hell didn't freeze over, but they began pulling out the long johns in Detroit after Hasek informed the Red Wings that he was forfeiting about $3 million of his $6-million salary in February 2004. The snowballs-chance-in-hell scenario came after Hasek injured his groin and announced an end to his season. "He just felt that he wasn't doing what he had really set out to do, which is to play hockey and play at a high level," said Detroit GM Ken Holland. Hasek played only 14 games in 2003–04. "I think it's an unbelievable gesture," noted Holland.

Largest investment loss
$5 million: Mike Modano, Dallas, 2003

Modano never revealed how big a hit he took, but according to *Sports Illustrated*, the Dallas Stars' scoring star lost "upwards of $5 million" in a bad investment. The setback preyed on Modano's mind and was a major factor in his slow start in 2003–04. As Modano told reporters in a November 2003 interview: "You put trust in people and it doesn't work out. That was a real hard thing for me to swallow and understand. It took some time for me to figure out that I couldn't do anything about it and just let it go. But I have."

Most money spent by a team picking up part of a traded player's contract

$20 million: Washington Capitals, January 23, 2004
Ignoring the advice of his hockey advisors, Capitals owner
Ted Leonsis opened the vault to land free agent Jaromir Jagr.
The $77-million, seven-year deal that Jagr signed in July 2001
made him the highest-paid player in history. The moody
Czech did little to justify the money Washington paid him,
however, and after only two and a half seasons he was dealt
to the Rangers. The key to the deal was Washington agreeing
to pick up a reported $20 million of the remaining $44 million
on Jagr's contract.

Longest personal-service contract signed by a player

21 years: Wayne Gretzky, Edmonton, Janaury 28, 1979
The contract that Gretzky signed with Oilers owner Peter
Pocklington was the longest in hockey history. Worth between
Cdn$4 and $5 million, the pact was inked at centre ice at North-
lands Coliseum on Gretzky's 18th birthday in front of 12,000
fans. Nine years later, Gretzky and Pocklington parted company
when the Great One was traded to Los Angeles.

Longest contract holdout

17 months: Nikolai Khabibulin, 1999 to 2001
The Siberian goalie spurned a $9-million, three-year contract
offer from Phoenix before the 1999–2000 season, then went into
hibernation. Nearly two full seasons later, on March 5, 2001,
Phoenix traded Khabibulin to Tampa Bay, who rewarded him for
his stubborness with a three-year $14.75-million deal.

First goalie from a Stanley Cup champion to stage a holdout
Ken Dryden, Montreal, 1973–74

After winning the Cup in 1973, Dryden locked horns with GM Sam Pollock over his Cdn$78,000-a-year contract. Dryden claimed he was getting shafted by the Canadiens, stating, "I can name six goaltenders who were higher paid than me last year." Dryden's threat was real. He announced he would sit out the upcoming season. Pollock called his bluff and the goalie began articling at a Toronto law firm for a paltry $135 a week. After the Habs were eliminated in the 1974 quarterfinals by the Rangers, Pollock coaxed Dryden back into the fold with a deal worth Cdn$200,000 a year.

First GM to ask a player to return a bonus payment
Kevin Lowe, Edmonton, December 2003

When Edmonton Oilers GM Kevin Lowe failed to come to terms on a new contract with holdout centre Mike Comrie prior to the 2003–04 season, relations between the two sides became frosty. In December, Lowe and Anaheim GM Bryan Murray tentatively agreed on a trade involving the Oilers holdout, and the Ducks and Comrie hammered out a two-year deal worth $1.65 million a year. But then Lowe changed his mind. He said he wouldn't trade Comrie unless the player paid the Oilers $2.5 million "to top up the deal." Comrie's agent, Rich Winter, called it "extortion," but the Oilers felt they were owed something by the departing centre, whose bonus-laden deal had earned him $7 million over the previous two and half years. The Anaheim deal collapsed when Comrie refused to cough up. A week later, the Oilers traded Comrie to the Flyers for Jeff Woywitka and two draft picks. This time, Lowe didn't ask for a bag of cash on the side.

Most money bid for a date with an NHL player

$12,500: Pavel Bure, Florida, February 17, 2001

As part of the Florida Panthers' 2001 charity fundraiser, team scoring star Pavel Bure agreed to be auctioned off as a dinner date to the highest bidder. When the bidding stalled at $6,500, Bure's date at the event, Russian tennis babe Anna Kournikova, hopped up on stage in a slinky, strapless dress that was slit to the thigh, and offered to include herself in the deal. Within moments the price of dinner rocketed to $12,500.

Most successful retail chain founded by a hockey player

Tim Hortons: Tim Horton, 1964

Few could imagine in 1964 that a small donut and coffee shop on Ottawa Street in Hamilton, Ontario, would be the start of a giant Canadian chain. "Always Fresh" was Horton and Ron Joyce's formula for success. Joyce was the store's first franchisee and became the hockey legend's full partner in 1967. After Horton was killed in a car accident in 1974, Joyce grew the business from a 40-shop chain into a 2,500-store operation employing 55,000.

Most money reportedly stolen by an NHL owner

$3.1 billion: John Rigas, Buffalo, 2002

The 77-year-old owner of the Buffalo Sabres and Adelphia Communications was charged with multiple counts of fraud in July 2002 for looting Adelphia on a massive scale and using the company as his family's personal piggy bank at the expense of the public investors and creditors. Rigas and his two sons, Timothy and Michael, faced up to 95 years in prison if convicted for their roles in what the U.S. Securities and Exchange Commission described as "one of the most extensive financial frauds ever to take place at a public company." After Rigas's arrest, the NHL assumed operational control of the Sabres franchise.

Largest owner fine for an altercation with a fan

$100,000: Ted Leonsis, Washington, January 2004

Leonsis is known for being a fan-friendly owner who personally
answers his e-mails and frequently greets fans at the MCI Center.
But after a 4–1 loss to Philadelphia in January 2004, the Capitals
owner and vice-chairman of America Online blew a fuse. He
attacked a 20-year-old fan named Jason Hammer, who had
led a derisive chant directed toward the owner during the game
while holding a sign that read: "Caps Hockey; AOL Stock—See
a Pattern?" According to news reports, Leonsis began choking
Hammer and security guards had to intervene. Leonsis later
apologized and invited Hammer to watch the next game
from his private box. The NHL fined Leonsis $100,000 for his
actions—not exactly what the doctor ordered, as the Caps
were already facing a $30-million deficit in 2003–04.

Largest player fine for an altercation with a fan
$53,658: Matthew Barnaby, Pittsburgh, December 2000

Moments after losing a fight to Florida's Peter Worrell, Barnaby was
given a gross misconduct when he grabbed the arm of 55-year-old
Keith Hubbell. The fan at National Car Rental Center in Sunrise,
Florida, had heckled Barnaby as the winger walked below him in
the runway that leads to the locker room. "All I said was 'How many
fingers am I holding up?' because he had one eye closed and looked
a little beat up," Hubbell told the *Miami Herald*, indicating how he
held two fingers up. "Maybe he thought I was shooting him the bird."
The NHL suspended Barnaby without pay for four games, a penalty
that cost him nearly $54,000.

First goalie to attempt to sell advertising space on his pads

Grant Fuhr, Edmonton, 1989

During a bitter contract wrangle with Oilers GM Glen Sather in the summer of 1989, Fuhr's agent, Rich Winter, announced that his client would retire if the NHL and the Oilers did not agree to a special waiver of the league's rules on licensing rights. Why? Winter had cut a five-year deal with Pepsi-Cola that called for Fuhr to wear the Pepsi logo on his goalie pads. The impasse was finally resolved in a meeting between Sather and Fuhr, at which the goalie agreed to report to training camp. Winter continued to argue that the NHL had no right to ban the Pepsi pads, but Fuhr soon lost interest in the issue. He lost interest in Winter, too, whom he later fired.

Most precious piece of hockey equipment deliberately destroyed

Georges Vezina's goalie pads, 2000

As a sales gimmick, snippets of the pads worn by Vezina during his celebrated career were affixed to 320 randomly inserted hockey cards in the 2000–01 Be A Player Ultimate Memorabilia set. The odds of a customer getting a card with a scrap of Vezina's gear were one in 2,400. The antique pads, which were put through a shredder after being acquired by company president Brian Price from a private collector, were thought to be the only ones in existence. In fact, Vezina artifacts are so rare that the Hockey Hall of Fame owns only a pair of the legendary goaltender's skates.

Most valuable hockey card

$20,000: Bert Corbeau, V145–1, 1923–24

Forget Bobby Orr or Gordie Howe rookie cards—that's kid stuff. The king of the collectibles market is a card featuring an obscure defenseman nicknamed "Pig Iron" from the 1923–24 Toronto St. Pats. Corbeau's card is highly valued because of its scarcity. Only 10 are known to exist.

Highest asking price for a hockey stick

$2 million: Gord Sharpe, 2001
$1 million: Mark O'Connell, 2004

Peterborough's Gord Sharpe knew he had something special when he was handed a very old hockey stick by the family of its original owner and maker, Alexander Rutherford Sr. of Lindsay, Ontario. The single piece of hand-carved hickory was analyzed by the Hockey Hall of Fame and dated to 1852. It proved to be the world's oldest hockey stick, so Sharpe offered it on eBay's Web site for a startling $2 million. He got no takers. Despite this, Mark O'Connell of Beaverton, Ontario, wasn't dissuaded from trying to sell his own metre-long relic of hockey history. After discovering an old stick in his cottage attic in 1990, O'Connell had let his son Kelly use it to play road hockey—until he heard about Sharpe's auction. According to historians, the faded black script stamped on the stick's blade (which reads "Ditson") means the stick was probably made before 1871. The weathered piece of wood, which more closely resembles a field-hockey stick, is considered one of the oldest mass-produced hockey sticks in existence.

Most personal insurance of a concussed player

$20 million: Eric Lindros, 2000–01

Lindros's personal insurance premium called for a $20-million payoff if an injury limited him to fewer than 20 games in 2000–01. The multi-concussed forward never claimed the payment, however, because he found himself without a place to play that year, a victim of the waiting game imposed by Philadelphia

GM Bob Clarke and a market limited to the few teams who could afford him.

Most money earned from stitches

$3,200: Bill Gadsby, 1946–47 to 1965–66

Gadsby had a classic hockey face, battered and lined with the 640 stitches he acquired during a 20-year NHL career. Painful as it was, the needlework had a side benefit, however. The rugged defenseman was one of the few players to take out insurance on potential cuts, which paid him $5 for every suture he received.

Most money lost by a player because of video replay
$500,000: Pavol Demitra, St. Louis, April 18, 1999

During the Blues' last regular-season game of 1998–99, Demitra needed one point to hit the 90-point plateau and activate a $500,000 bonus in his contract. Demitra's half-million dollars was all but deposited in the bank when he assisted on a goal by Lubos Bartecko. Unfortunately, a video replay revealed that Bartecko was in the crease, a violation of the rules. The goal was cancelled as quickly as the $500,000 check. Interestingly, another opportunity came late in the game, with St. Louis leading Los Angeles 3–2. Rather than score into an open net though, Demitra fed the puck to linemate Scott Young, who was one goal shy of the 25 he needed to collect on his own $300,000 bonus. Yet neither man benefitted, as Young's shot was blocked by defenseman Jaroslav Modry.

Most money dumped in a fire sale

$32.8 million: Washington Capitals, 2003–04
$25.1 million: New York Rangers, 2003–04

In a unique scenario created by parity among playoff contenders and uncertainty over the pending collective bargaining agreement with the Players' Association, New York and Washington started chopping payrolls by unloading high-priced talent at the 2004 trading deadline. Both clubs were underachieving and had little chance of making the postseason. The Capitals moved out Jaromir Jagr, Robert Lang, Peter Bondra, Sergei Gonchar, Anson Carter, Michael Nylander, Mike Grier and, earlier, Steve Konowalchuk—eight of their top-10 salaries. Washington began the season ninth out of 30 teams in terms of payroll, but ranked 26th after the fire sale. The Rangers trimmed their payroll from $74.5 to $49.4 million by dealing Brian Leetch, Petr Nedved, Alexei Kovalev and others.

Worst $100 never spent by a team
New York Rangers, 1943

In 1943, the Rangers invited a 15-year-old kid from Floral, Saskatchewan, named Gordie Howe, to a tryout camp in Winnipeg. Rangers GM Lester Patrick was impressed enough by what he saw of Howe to offer him $100 to sign a form that would have made him Rangers property. But Howe, who was in Grade 8, declined, saying he was homesick and wanted to return home to his family and friends. A year later, the man who would become hockey's greatest scorer signed with Detroit.

Most mean-spirited lawsuit launched by an NHL team
Minnesota Wild, 2000

Greed has no bounds. Even before the expansion Minnesota Wild had played a single game, the club was already working on a power play. It filed a lawsuit against the children's magazine *Wild*, which had been published for five years by the Canadian

Wildlife Federation, demanding that the CWF give up its rights to the trademark so that the team could use the name "Wild" for its own marketing and promotion purposes. Lawyers for the NHL and the team also asked that the CWF be restricted in how it used the word "Wild" and that the federation pick up all legal costs for the court action. The CWF, a charitable operation that educates young people on the value of conservation while working to preserve wilderness and wildlife, was not amused. "It boggles my mind, the arrogance they display," said CWF executive vice-president Colin Maxwell. "Frankly, we'd like a little respect and we'd like a little courtesy. Taking such extreme action before approaching us directly is like swatting a fly with a hammer."

Most money spent per win, one season

$2.65 million: New York Rangers, 2003–04
$2.11 million: New York Rangers, 1999–2000

Money certainly didn't buy happiness for the Rangers, who finished with near identical results in 1999–2000 and 2003–04 after spending more than the gross national product of some countries. Apparently, New York learned nothing after blowing $2.11 million per win with a 29–38–12–3 record in 1999–2000. That number ballooned to $2.65 million per win in 2003–04, even after the Blueshirts slashed their $74.5–million payroll to $49.4 million at the trade deadline.

Largest team debt

$100 million: Pittsburgh Penguins, 1998

This was the sum that Penguins owners Roger Marino and Harold Baldwin claimed the team owed when they declared bankruptcy on October 13, 1998. Among the lengthy list of creditors was Penguins superstar Mario Lemieux. A year later,

Lemieux acquired control of the club in a bid to make back the
millions owed to him.

Most costly act of civil unrest related to hockey

Cdn$50,000, The Richard Riot, Montreal, March 17, 1955
The animosity between league officials and Maurice Richard
had been building for years. Finally, in a fight against Boston
defenseman Hal Laycoe on March 13, 1955, Richard pushed
too far. After some stickwork between the players, the fiery
Richard punched linesman Cliff Thompson in the face. NHL
President Clarence Campbell suspended the Rocket for the
final three games of 1954–55 and the playoffs. At the next
Montreal Forum game, a tear-gas bomb exploded. The game
was cancelled and rioting spilled out onto the Montreal streets.
Downtown stores were looted, several police cars damaged
and dozens arrested in the subsequent mayhem. Glass and
debris littered Montreal's main business street, St. Catherine,
for 20 city blocks. Only radio and television appeals by Richard
quieted the city. The damage and "wholesale looting of shops"
was estimated at Cdn$50,000.

CHAPTER 7

My Face
is my mask

Gump Worsley holds the record for
most regular-season games played
without a mask: 855. In fact, Worsley didn't don a
face protector until the last six games of his 21st
and final season. The feat is even more remarkable
when we consider the rain of rubber directed at the
Gumper during his 10 hellish years with the Rangers.
When asked why he didn't wear one, Worsley
offered his classic reply: "My face *is* my mask."

Only goalie employed by the NHL rather than a team

Wilf Cude, 1931 32

Born in Wales and raised in Winnipeg, Cude made the big time in 1930–31 with the Philadelphia Quakers. When the Quakers suspended operations after the season ended, he was signed as a backup goalie—not by another team but by the NHL itself. On call in case of emergency, Cude played two games for Boston and one for Chicago. The rest of the time he tended net for the Boston Cubs of the Can-Am League.

Oddest contractual arrangement made by a goalie
Jimmy Franks, Detroit, 1943–44

Franks, who should have been nicknamed "Hot Dog," was a career minor leaguer until Detroit loaned him to the Rangers as a temporary wartime replacement in 1942–43. Convinced that his 4.48 GAA in 23 games with the last-place Blueshirts proved that he belonged in the big leagues, the 28-year-old refused a demotion to the minors the next fall. Detroit slapped Franks with a suspension in October, but lifted it two months later and allowed him to rejoin the team after he agreed to play road games only.

Only goalie to make his NHL debut because the starter had to use the bathroom

Randy Exelby, Montreal, January 27, 1989

Exelby was Montreal's backup goalie during a game against Buffalo, when starter Patrick Roy suddenly left the ice and rushed to the dressing room. A buzz went through the Montreal Forum. Was Roy injured? Not exactly. As it turned out, he had a powerful need to use the men's room. Exelby subbed for two minutes and 55 seconds, making one save, before Roy returned. The brief stint gave Exelby the record for the shortest NHL career of any goalie, a distinction that he forfeited the following year when he played a full 60 minutes for Edmonton.

Only goalie to admit to intentionally letting in goals

Hec Fowler, Boston, December 22, 1924

We'll never know if Fowler was telling the truth, but Boston coach and GM Art Ross didn't care. On December 22, 1924, Ross yanked Fowler from the net during the third period of a 10–1 pasting by Toronto and replaced him with defenseman George Redding. Coach and goalie got into a heated debate after the game, and Fowler informed Ross that he let in a few goals intentionally to bring attention to just how poor a team Ross had assembled. Fowler was fined and suspended and never played in the NHL again.

Only goalie to miss a game because of injuries suffered in a previous life

Gilles Gratton, 1975–76 to 1976–77

A decidedly strange piece of work, Gratton believed in reincarnation and claimed his job of facing flying pucks was divine punishment for having stoned people to death during the Spanish Inquisition. Gratton's dedication didn't match his talent. He refused to play one night because the moon was in the wrong place in the sky. Another time, Gratton missed a start because he was feeling the effects of a sword wound that he had suffered 500 years earlier. "Grattoony the Loony" gave up hockey for good after three years in the WHA and two in the NHL.

Only third-string university goalie called up by an NHL team

Chris Levesque, Vancouver, December 9, 2003

Levesque thought his friends were joking when they pulled him out of a library at the University of British Columbia and told him the Vancouver Canucks needed him to play goal. It was no joke. Canucks starting goalie Dan Cloutier had been injured at the morning skate and, though the club had Johan Hedberg to replace him, it was unable to fly a minor-league backup into Vancouver in time for that night's game against Pittsburgh. So the club turned to the UBC Thunderbirds. Because UBC's top two goalies were ineligible, the Canucks had to sign Levesque, the third-stringer, to a one-game contract. Levesque, whom the Canucks nicknamed Eddie Lebec after the hapless goalie on *Cheers,* suited up and sat on the bench. Even weirder, he almost got into the action. Late in the first period, Hedberg was creamed in a collision. As the trainer attended to the fallen goalie, TV cameras zoomed in on Levesque's face, which was rapidly draining of all colour. To the kid's relief, Hedberg, who fractured his wrist on the play, got up and finished the game.

Only goalie to win the last games played at the Montreal Forum and at Maple Leaf Gardens
Jocelyn Thibault, March 11, 1996 and February 13, 1999
No matter what he does the rest of his career, Thibault will be forever known as the goalie who won the last games played at Canada's two greatest hockey shrines. In 1996, he led the Canadiens to a 4–1 victory over the Dallas Stars in the final game at the Montreal Forum. Three years later, he backstopped the Chicago Blackhawks to a 6–2 triumph over Toronto in the curtain-closer at Maple Leaf Gardens.

Most impressive rookie season by an NHL goalie
Frank Brimsek, Boston, 1938–39
A number of netminders made a splash in their rookie seasons, but no one was as dominating as Brimsek in 1938–39. In the first

10 games of his career, the 22-year-old American registered six shutouts, including two scoreless streaks of 220-plus minutes. He went on to top the NHL with 10 shutouts, a league-best 1.56 goals-against average and a league-high 33 wins for the first-place Bruins. Brimsek was just as hot in the playoffs, posting a 1.25 GAA and leading Boston to its first Cup in a decade. He was voted a First Team All-Star and won both the Calder and Vezina Trophies. No rookie goalie has matched that performance.

First goalie to join the attack in the opposition zone
Charlie Rayner, NY Rangers, December 28, 1946
One of Rayner's ambitions was to score a goal in an NHL game, and in 1946–47, Rangers coach Frank Boucher was willing to let him try. Instead of pulling Rayner for an extra attacker during a faceoff in the Detroit end, with 35 seconds left and his team trailing 2–1, Boucher stationed his netminder just inside the Red Wings' blueline. Rayner didn't score, but teammate Hal Laycoe did, rifling the puck past Harry Lumley with seven seconds left. Five days later against Toronto, with the Rangers down 5–4 and less than a minute remaining, Boucher again sent Rayner to join the attack in the opposition zone. This time, New York failed to score. Boucher soon abandoned the bizarre strategy, but Rayner had left his mark.

First goalie to score a goal in junior hockey and in the NHL
Chris Osgood, 1991 and 1996
Five years separated Osgood's first two goals, which approximates the scoring rate of Ken Daneyko. He scored on January 3, 1991, with the Medicine Hat Tigers of the Western Hockey League, then repeated the feat on March 6, 1996, with the Detroit Red Wings.

First goalie to have his mask design censored
Ed Giacomin, Detroit, 1970s

After the Rangers traded him to the Motor City in the late-1970s, Giacomin signed an endorsement deal with Champion Spark Plugs. To give the company some prime-time exposure, Giacomin agreed to wear a "Spark with Eddie" logo on his mask. The NHL deep-sixed the idea, but Giacomin went ahead and kept the mask motif he had designed—two lightning bolts above the eye-holes.

Most loaned goalie
Abbie Cox, 1929–30 to 1935–36

Goalies are often known as loners, but Cox was a professional loaner. The career minor leaguer was loaned to NHL clubs to replace injured netminders five times. During the 1930s, he made guest appearances for the Montreal Maroons, New York Americans, Detroit Red Wings and Montreal Canadiens.

Most consecutive 70-game seasons
7: Glenn Hall, 1952–53 to 1970–71
7: Martin Brodeur, 1991–92 to 2003–04

Fans are only beginning to grasp the full extent of the incredible numbers that Brodeur has been putting up. Between 1991–92 and 2003–04, the New Jersey puckstopper appeared in 649 of a possible 738 games.

Most consecutive starts, one season
76: Grant Fuhr, St. Louis, 1995–96

Mike Keenan used Fuhr like a plough horse in 1995–96, starting him in the first 76 games of the season. Keenan may even have intended to start his goalie in all 82 of the Blues' games, but Fuhr hurt his knee in Game 76 and had to sit out a few. Was this a wise strategy with a 33-year-old goalie who had played only 17 games the previous year? Probably not. Fuhr reinjured his knee in the playoffs and the Blues were forced to use backup Jon Casey.

Most seasons leading the league in wins
6: Clint Benedict, 1917–18 to 1929–30
6: Martin Brodeur, 1991–92 to 2003–04
Benedict paced the NHL in wins in six straight seasons with the Ottawa Senators from 1918–19 to 1923–24. Brodeur has led the league in wins six times in seven seasons, 1997–98 to 2003–04. During that span, only Detroit's Dominik Hasek, in 2001–02, managed to break Brodeur's stranglehold.

Fewest games to record 100 wins from start of career
139: Bill Durnan, 1943–44 to 1949–50
It took Durnan less than three years to reach 100 career wins. His record in that span was 100–23–16. Durnan was very good, but so too was his team: Montreal finished first in each of those three seasons. He reached the milestone in the second-last game of 1945–46.

Most combined wins for two teams, one season
34: Patrick Roy, Montreal and Colorado, 1995–96
34: Bill Ranford, Edmonton and Boston, 1995–96
Good goalies don't often switch postal codes in midseason. But these two did—and in the same season, no less. After posting 12 wins for Montreal, Roy was dealt to Colorado on December 6, 1995, where he recorded 22. After getting 13 victories for Edmonton, Ranford was traded to Boston, where he picked up 21.

Largest margin by a league leader in wins

21: Bill Durnan, Montreal, 1943–44
17: Tiny Thompson, Boston, 1929–30
17: Terry Sawchuk, Detroit, 1950–51

The Canadiens tore up the league in 1943–44, posting a 38–5–7 record. Durnan, who started all 50 of Montreal's games, won 38, an amazing 21 more than his closest competitors: Detroit's Connie Dion and Boston's Bert Gardiner. Thompson and Sawchuk also profited from playing for superior teams. Thompson won 38 games with the Bruins in a 44-game schedule in 1929–30, while Sawchuk won 44 games for Detroit in a 70-game schedule in 1950–51.

Lowest winning percentage, career (min. 250 decisions)

.353: Ron Low, 1972–73 to 1984–85
.366: Bill Beveridge, 1929–30 to 1942–43
.367: Dunc Wilson, 1969–70 to 1978–79

Low is right. After logging net duty in three cities with three pathetic teams (Toronto, Washington and Detroit), Low was dealt to the up and coming Edmonton Oilers in 1980 and got to experience his first taste of winning. But it didn't last. In 1983, a year before Edmonton won its first Cup, Low was traded to New Jersey, the league's cesspool, where he ended his career. His final numbers were 102–203–38.

Most games without a win, career

21: Mike O'Neill, 1991–92 to 1996–97

Virtually no one remembers O'Neill, and he may prefer it that way. Shuttling back and forth between the minors, he failed to post a single win in 21 NHL appearances (20 of them with the Winnipeg Jets and one with the Anaheim Mighty Ducks in the 1990s). O'Neill's official line was 0–9–2.

Most games without a win, one season

35: Michel Belhumeur, Washington, 1974–75

Tending net for the Capitals in 1974–75 was a nightmarish task: the outgunned expansion club allowed an NHL-record 446 goals. First-stringer Ron Low posted a woeful 5.45 GAA in 48 games, while backup Belhumeur had a miserable 5.36 GAA in 35 games. The biggest difference between the two was in the win column. Low won eight games; Belhumeur won zero and finished the season with a 0–24–3 record. Belhumeur never did win a game with the Caps or another game in the NHL. The next year, he had a 0–5–1 mark when he was demoted to the minors.

Most losses by a rookie goalie, one season
39: Ken McAuley, NY Rangers 1943–44
34: Gerry Desjardins, Los Angeles, 1968–69

McAuley got his NHL shot with a war-ravaged Rangers club in 1943–44 and had a record-setting season. Unfortunately, all the records he set were for futility: worst GAA in a season (6.24), most goals allowed in a season (310) and most losses by a rookie (39).

Most consecutive seasons with a goals-against average under 2.00

5: Terry Sawchuk, 1950–51 to 1954–55

Sawchuk staked his claim to being the greatest goaltender of all time in his first five NHL campaigns. With machine-like consistency, he rattled off a series of mind-boggling GAA numbers: 1.99, 1.90, 1.90, 1.93 and 1.96. In each of the five seasons, he also topped the league in wins and three times led in shutouts. After Sawchuk backstopped Detroit to its second straight Stanley Cup in 1955, Red Wings GM Jack Adams mysteriously traded his star goalie to Boston, where his average rose to 2.60 with the fifth-place Bruins.

Most goals allowed by a goalie employed by the U.S. Air Force, one game
6: Don Aiken, Montreal, March 13, 1958

Being a backup NHL goalie wasn't a full-time job in the 1950s. A native of Arlington, Massachussets, Aiken worked as a mathematician with the U.S. Air Force while doing double duty as the Boston Bruin's practice goalie. He was loaned to Montreal after starter Jacques Plante was knocked cold midway through a game against Boston in 1958, and proved to be the Bruins' secret weapon. The overmatched amateur allowed six goals in a 7–3 Boston win.

Most goals allowed, one period
9: Bunny Larocque, Toronto, March 19, 1981

Larocque was billed as a saviour when Toronto acquired the four-time Cup winner from the Canadiens on March 10, 1981. But tending net for the lowly Leafs wasn't quite as simple as it had been in Montreal. Only nine days after the trade, Larocque experienced the worst 20 minutes of any goalie in NHL history when he was scorched for nine goals by the Buffalo Sabres in the second period of a 14–4 blowout. Larocque lasted less than two years in Toronto, posting a fat 4.79 GAA in 74 games.

Most consecutive seasons recording a shutout
19: Terry Sawchuk, 1949–50 to 1967–68

They called him the Shutout King. The nickname was richly deserved. Sawchuk failed to post a zero in only one season of his 21-year career: his 20th with Detroit, in 1968–69. His best single-season shutout tally was 12, which he reached three times in the 1950s.

Most games by a goalie who recorded only one shutout, career
207: John Garrett, 1979–80 to 1984–85

At least Garrett can say that he was perfect once. He registered his lone NHL zero with the Vancouver Canucks in a 3–0 win over the Winnipeg Jets on March 2, 1983. After the game, teammate Tiger Williams took the trainer's scissors and snipped out a chunk of the twine as a souvenir for his goalie.

Fewest games played by a goalie who recorded a shutout, career
2: Joe Ironstone, 1925–26 to 1927–28

Ironstone's name was longer than his career, which consisted of a 40-minute stint in relief for the New York Americans in 1925–26 and one full game for the Toronto Maple Leafs against Boston on March 3, 1928. Ironstone was recruited by Leafs GM Conn Smythe the day of the game to replace injured John Ross Roach. He blanked the first-place Bruins in a 0–0 overtime draw, but reportedly made an enemy of Smythe by refusing to don the pads unless the GM raised his fee. Ironstone continued to play until 1936, but never got another shot in the NHL.

Most games before recording a shutout from start of career
175: Ed Staniowski, 1975–76 to 1984–85
170: Jeff Hackett, 1988–89 to 2003–04

A backup for most of his NHL career, Staniowski didn't get a chance to play regularly until his seventh season with the Winnipeg Jets. On March 20, 1982, he recorded his first shutout in his 176th game as Winnipeg whipped Toronto 7–0. Staniowski ended his career with two shutouts in 219 games.

Most shutouts in back-to-back seasons

35: George Hainsworth, Montreal, 1927–28 and 1928–29

In the late 1920s, scoring in the NHL declined to an all-time low. If a team counted three goals in a game it was considered a windfall. Goalkeepers never had it so easy. Hainsworth, who tended net for the first-place Canadiens, recorded 13 shutouts in 1927–28 and 22 in 1928–29. That's 35 goose eggs in 88 games.

MODERN-DAY RECORD

24: Bernie Parent, Philadelphia, 1973–74 and 1974–75

For all the attention the Flyers received for their goon-squad tactics, they would not have won the Stanley Cup if not for the Frenchman with the white mask. Parent was king of the crease in 1973–74 and 1974–75, posting a league-high 12 shutouts each season and winning two Vezina Trophies. He continued his sterling play in the postseason, capturing back-to-back Conn Smythe Trophies.

Age of youngest shutout leader
20.I years: Tom Barrasso, Buffalo, 1984–85
21.2 years: Terry Sawchuk, Detroit, 1950–5I

Considering how good Barrasso was as a youngster, he should have enjoyed an even better career than he did. In his second NHL season, the Sabres goalie displayed the poise of a seasoned vet. Although he only turned 20 a week before the end of the season, he led the NHL with five shutouts—no other goalie posted more than two that year—and also had a league-leading 2.66 GAA.

Age of oldest shutout leader

37.5 years: Glenn Hall, St. Louis, 1968–69

37.2 years: Georges Vezina, Montreal, 1923–24

Age didn't seem to be a deterrent for Hall. Sharing the Blues' netminding workload with his even more ancient partner, Jacques Plante, the 37-year-old Hall logged eight shutouts in 41 games to lead all netminders in 1968–69.

Fewest shutouts by a league leader

ALL-TIME RECORD

1: Georges Vezina, Montreal, 1917–18

1: Clint Benedict, Ottawa, 1917–18

Vezina and Benedict notched the only two shutouts in the NHL's inaugural season. Vezina was the first, picking up his zero on February 18, 1918, as the Canadiens clobbered Toronto 9–0. Benedict backstopped Ottawa to an 8–0 win over Vezina's Canadiens on February 25, 1918.

MODERN-DAY RECORD

3: Don Edwards, Buffalo, 1980–81

3: Chico Resch, NY Islanders/Colorado, 1980–81

3: Denis Herron, Montreal, 1981–82

In the early 1980s, the shutout was on the endangered species list. For two straight seasons, no NHL netminder logged more than three.

Only goalie to record more shutouts than the rest of league

Johnny Mowers, Detroit, 1942–43

Here's another one from the unbreakable files. Mowers won the Vezina Trophy and notched six zeros for the Red Wings. The rest of the league's wartime goalies managed to produce a total of five. With Mowers holding the fort, Detroit finished first and won the Cup. After the season, Mowers enlisted in the Royal

Canadian Air Force. Although he tried to make a comeback after the war, the game had passed him by. He never won another NHL game.

Most shutouts by a goalie on a last-place team

7: Charlie Rayner, NY Rangers, 1948–49
6: Hap Holmes, Detroit, 1926–27
6: Ed Johnston, Boston, 1963–64

A great talent, who had the misfortune of playing on a lot of bad teams, Rayner credited his development as a goalie to the teachings of Eddie Shore, his coach with Springfield in the American Hockey League in the early 1940s. Rayner's seven shutouts in 1948–49 ranked second behind the total of Montreal's Bill Durnan, who had 10.

Most shutouts in a final season
15: Hal Winkler, Boston, 1927–28

Despite Winkler's league-leading 15 shutouts and stingy 1.51 GAA, Boston believed it could improve its goaltending situation by replacing the 36-year-old veteran with 22-year-old rookie Tiny Thompson. Winkler went to the minors and Thompson led the Bruins to the Cup in 1928–29. Even so, Winkler's 15 shutouts remains a Boston record.

Longest shutout sequence
MODERN-DAY RECORD

332:01: Brian Boucher, Phoenix, December 22, 2003 to January 11, 2004
309:21: Bill Durnan, Montreal, February 24, 1949 to March 9, 1949
245:33: Turk Broda, Toronto, October 15, 1950 to October 29, 1950

The odds that any goalie might break Bill Durnan's modern-day record of five consecutive shutouts were at least 10,000 to one. But for Boucher they were even higher. At the start of 2003–04, his NHL career seemed to be nearing an end. Third on the depth chart in Phoenix behind Sean Burke and Zac Bierk, he had been put on waivers earlier in the season by the Coyotes—and no one claimed him. But when injuries opened up a spot in midseason, the 26-year-old seized the opportunity. Boucher blanked opponents in an amazing five straight games before a deflected shot by Randy Robitaille got past him at 6:16 of the first period of his next start, a 1–1 tie with the Atlanta Thrashers. Boucher's shutout streak ended 129 minutes and 28 seconds short of the all-time record set by Ottawa's Alex Connell in the dead-puck days of 1927–28.

Only goalie to shut out his own team in his first NHL game
Claude Pronovost, Boston, January 14, 1956
An odd twist of fate caused Pronovost to make his NHL debut with Boston rather than with the team that owned him, the Montreal Canadiens. When Bruins starter Terry Sawchuk went down with an injury, Boston called up "Long" John Henderson from its AHL affiliate, the Hershey Bears. Henderson arrived in time for the Saturday night tilt at the Montreal Forum, but his equipment got lost in transit. Henderson, who stood six foot one, couldn't find any other gear that fit. To help out, the Canadiens loaned the Bruins Pronovost, the backup goalie with the Montreal Royals of the Quebec Hockey League, as an emergency replacement. The 20-year-old stopped 31 shots and led Boston to a 2–0 win over the first-place Habs, earning a loud ovation from the Montreal fans. It was the lone shutout of Pronovost's three-game NHL career.

Most shutouts by two goalies on the same team, one season

16: Roy Worters and Flat Walsh, NY Americans, 1928–29

This record should really bear the names of a modern-day goalie tandem; instead it is held by two old-timers from an era when teams never carried backups. Walsh, who was the property of the Montreal Maroons, was loaned to the Americans because newly acquired Worters had been suspended by the league for refusing to report after his trade from Pittsburgh. Once the matter was cleared up (after a special Board of Governors meeting), Worters donned his pads. That left Walsh out of a job after just four games, but his three shutouts earned him a spot in the record books. Worters compiled 13 zeros that year.

Age of youngest goalie to record a shutout

18.2 years: Harry Lumley, Detroit, January 14, 1945
18.9 years: Tom Barrasso, Buffalo, January 18, 1984
18.11 years: Marc-Andre Fleury, Pittsburgh, October 30, 2003

Lumley, who at age 17 became the youngest goalie to play in an NHL game, also holds this less-known record. At 18 years, 65 days, the Red Wings rookie stoned Toronto 3–0 to pick up his lone shutout of the 1944–45 season.

Age of oldest NHL goalie to record a shutout

44 years, 66 days: Jacques Plante, Boston, March 24, 1973
44 years, 34 days: Johnny Bower, Toronto, December 12, 1968

This is geezer country. Not many goalies are still playing at age 44, much less posting NHL shutouts. But Plante turned aside 29 shots as Boston beat the Rangers 3–0, allowing Plante to beat Bower's old-man mark by 32 days. The 44-year-old Maple Leafs great made 27 stops for his last zero in a 1–0 win over the Philadelphia Flyers.

Most shots faced by a winning goalie, one game
68: Jake Forbes, NY Americans, December 26, 1925
68: Mario Lessard, Los Angeles, March 24, 1981

Forbes is credited with facing 68 shots in a 3–1 Americans win over the Pittsburgh Pirates, but you really have to doubt the accuracy of his total, since scorekeeping was a haphazard science in hockey's early days. Lessard was pelted with 68 shots as Los Angeles defeated the Minnesota North Stars 4–3. Lessard led the NHL with 35 wins that season—no small accomplishment considering the porous Kings' defense.

First alternating goalie tandem
Chuck Rayner and Sugar Jim Henry, NY Rangers, 1945–46

New York Rangers coach Frank Boucher had a flair for off-the-cuff innovation, especially with his goalies. In an era in which all teams carried only one netminder, Boucher began 1946–47 with two: Chuck Rayner and Sugar Jim Henry, whom he alternated between the pipes from game to game. Boucher stuck with that routine until a tilt in Toronto on November 24, 1945. In that game, Rayner caught a stick in the face in the first period and had to leave to get sewn up. Rather than wait for him to return, Boucher simply sent Henry over the boards. When Rayner returned a few minutes later, Boucher sent him in to replace Henry. The two netminders stopped at the blueline and swapped sticks and gloves. Boucher liked the idea so much that he kept switching his goalies the rest of the game after every third shift—and every time the two men exchanged gear. Did it pay dividends? Not exactly. The Leafs won 4–3. After the game, reporters thought it strange that the Rangers could afford two goalies but only one goalie stick.

Most five-or-more-goal games allowed to individual players, career

4: Howard Lockhart, 1919–20 to 1924–25

Lockhart's nickname was Holes, which is exactly what opposing shooters found in him. He gave up five goals to Hamilton's Mickey Roach during the 1919–20 season when the Toronto St. Pats loaned him to the Quebec Bulldogs for a game. Lockhart joined Roach in Hamilton the following year, where he perfected the sieve act, surrendering six-goal games to both Cy and Corbett Denneny and a five-goal game to Newsy Lalonde.

Last goalie to allow five goals by one player, one game

Jim Carey, Washington, December 26, 1996

In today's game, a goaltender usually gets the hook before he allows five goals in a game, much less five to one player. But in this instance, Carey still had a chance to get the win: the Capitals and Wings were tied 4–4 after 60 minutes in this Boxing Day clash at the Joe Louis Arena. Unfortunately for Carey, his nemesis, Sergei Fedorov, wasn't content with four goals. The Detroit gunner reloaded and ended the show in overtime with his fifth bullet of the game.

CHAPTER 8

Locked
and loaded

Who do you call when you need a goal? In 2000–01, the Florida Panthers kept calling on explosive right-winger Pavel Bure, who scored a league-high 59 goals. Not only did the Russian Rocket's 59 goals set a new Florida record, they represented 29.5 per cent of the Panthers' total output for the season, the highest percentage in NHL history.

Fastest first NHL goal

15 seconds: Gus Bodnar, Toronto, October 30, 1943
18 seconds: Danny Gare, Buffalo, October 10, 1974
20 seconds: Alexander Mogilny, Buffalo, October 5, 1989
Every NHL player has a shot at breaking Bodnar's record—but
only one. The 20-year-old centre had a remarkable debut, picking up two goals and an assist in Toronto's 5–2 opening-night
win over the New York Rangers in 1943. His first goal was scored
after just 15 seconds, an NHL record that still stands. Bodnar
also had a stellar season, collecting a rookie record 62 points
on 22 goals and 40 assists. He won the Calder Trophy easily,
attracting far more votes than Montreal Canadiens rookie goalie
Bill Durnan, who was 38–5–7 with a league-leading 2.18 GAA.

Fastest first NHL point
**12 seconds: Bobby Carpenter, Washington,
October 7, 1981**
The Capitals' number one draft pick in 1981 made his debut with
Washington at age 18 against the Buffalo Sabres. Carpenter assisted
on a goal by Ryan Walter just 12 seconds after the opening faceoff.
No other rookie has ever gotten on the scoreboard so quickly.

Fastest first goal by an NHL superstar

1:41: Mario Lemieux, Pittsburgh, October 11, 1984
On his very first NHL shift, the 19-year-old Lemieux intercepted
a Ray Bourque pass near centre ice and took off like a thousand
times before in pond hockey and junior play. In alone, with
Bourque in pursuit, Lemieux swooped down on Boston's Pete
Peeters, drawing the goalie to his knees with a sharp shift and
snapping a backhand into the twine. Lemieux played unremark-

ably for the next two months (no goals), but his first goal gave everyone pause: a new gun was in town, so look out.

Most enthusiastic fan response to a player's first NHL goal
Bobby Orr, Boston, October 23, 1966
Orr posted his first NHL goal in his second game on October 27, 1966, drilling a point shot past Montreal goalie Gump Worsley. The unassisted tally, at 4:13 of the third period, drew a long and loud standing ovation from the fans at Boston Garden, who realized they were witnessing the dawn of a new era in Beantown.

Only player whose lone NHL goal was a franchise first
Morris Stefaniw, Atlanta Flames, October 7, 1972
Stefaniw's lone NHL goal was memorable because it was the first in Atlanta Flames history. The milestone marker came at 12:48 of the first period of the Flames' first game, a 3–2 victory over the New York Islanders. Stefaniw played 13 games with Atlanta before being sent to the minors. He never returned.

Age of youngest player to score an NHL goal
16.11 years: Bep Guidolin, Boston, November 24, 1942
Called up from junior as a wartime replacement player, Guidolin was two weeks shy of his 17th birthday when he scored his first NHL goal against Chicago goalie Bert Gardiner. The goal came in the teenager's second NHL game and was his first before the hometown fans in Boston. (Guidolin actually made his debut 12 days earlier against Toronto, but had trouble obtaining the proper travel documents to cross the border.)

Age of youngest player to score an NHL goal (since 1945)
18.1 years: Grant Mulvey, Chicago, October 19, 1974
Mulvey was 18 years, one month and two days old when he

notched his first NHL goal against St. Louis. Patrick Marleau was two days older than Mulvey when he scored for the San Jose Sharks in a 5–3 loss to Phoenix on October 19, 1997, exactly 23 years to the day after Mulvey's goal.

Age of youngest player to score a regular-season overtime goal

18.5 years: Steve Yzerman, Detroit, October 26, 1983
The Red Wings rookie scored his second goal of the night, stuffing a rebound past goalie Bob Sauve with 22 seconds left in overtime to give Detroit a 6–5 win over the Sabres. At 18 years, 170 days, Yzerman was already a go-to guy in Detroit.

Age of oldest player to score his first NHL goal

37.4 years: Helmut Balderis, Minnesota, November 2, 1989
One of the flashiest Soviet stars of the 1970s, Balderis was nicknamed Electruchka "Electric Train." However, by the time he joined the North Stars at age 37, in 1989, he had been retired for four years and his power had left him. Balderis, who scored his first NHL goal against Chicago, abandoned his comeback after logging nine points in 26 games.

Most game-winning goals, career

110: Brett Hull, 1985–86 to 2003–04
100: Phil Esposito, 1963–64 to 1980–81
97: Guy Lafleur, 1971–72 to 1990–91
Game-winning goals just don't get any respect as a bona fide stat. They are completely absent from the *NHL Guide* and, as a result, players are denied records as regular-season leaders. The numbers show Hull on top, for example, but that doesn't include game winners scored by players before the stat was first compiled in 1967–68. As well, Esposito has 100 game-winning goals, but how many did he get in his four seasons before 1967–68?

Stats Inc. says another 18, which would beat Hull. Then there is Gordie Howe. The 26-year NHL veteran decided to list his own numbers (if no one else would) in his bio, *Gordie Howe: My Hockey Memories*. According to the book, Howe tallied 188, which means that one in almost every four of his 802 career goals was a game winner.

Most consecutive game-winning goals from start of career
4: Artem Chubarov, Vancouver, 1999–2000 to 2001–02
An odd distinction to be sure. Even weirder, it was not until his third season that Chubarov notched a goal that wasn't a game winner. The Russian rookie scored once in 49 games with the Canucks in 1999–2000. He played only one game in his second year, then potted three more consecutive game winners in 2001–02 before the string ended.

Most game-winning goals in consecutive seasons
32: Phil Esposito, Boston, 1970–71 and 1971–72
Esposito was criticized for scoring a lot of "garbage" goals, but though other players may have been more artistic, no one was more effective at putting the biscuit in the basket. In fact, the league is still waiting for someone to break Esposito's mark of 16 game-winning goals in a season, which he set with the Bruins in 1970–71, then duplicated the next. For comparison's sake, Wayne Gretzky's personal high was 12 game winners and Mario Lemieux's best was 10.

Most game-winning goals by a rookie
9: Steve Larmer, Chicago, 1982–83
Although seven other rookies have scored more goals than Larmer did in his first season, no freshman has ever potted more

game winners. Nine of Larmer's 43 goals won games for Chicago in 1982–83.

Only player to score a game-winning goal after sneaking into the arena

Bill Sutherland, Philadelphia, October 19, 1967

Sutherland scored his first NHL goal and the first in Flyers history in a 5–1 loss to the Oakland Seals on October 11, 1967. But this flash of fame didn't raise the rookie's profile. In fact, Sutherland was forced to sneak into the Philadelphia Spectrum for the club's first home game after being refused entry by an usher who did not believe he was a player. Sutherland proceeded to score the Flyers' first goal at the Spectrum, which stood up as the game winner in a 1–0 victory over Pittsburgh.

Largest goals-to-assists differential, career (min. 300 goals)

133: Nels Stewart, 1925–26 to 1939–40
123: Maurice Richard, 1942–43 to 1959–60

Stewart reached the 20-goal mark nine times in an era when scoring 20 was a real accomplishment. When he retired in 1940, he had registered more goals than any NHLer, with a final tally of 324 goals and 191 assists. Stewart's record lasted until 1952, when Maurice Richard broke it. The Rocket finished with 544 goals and 421 assists.

Largest goals-to-assists differential, one season

41: Brett Hull, St. Louis, 1990–91
40: Joe Malone, Montreal, 1917–18
34: Lanny McDonald, Calgary, 1982–83

The Golden Brett ranks as one of the deadliest shooters to appear on an NHL rink. In 1990–91, he lit the lamp 86 times and added 45 assists for an astounding differential of 41. Hull owns three of the top five marks in the category. He also had two seasons with a 31-goal differential with the Blues. Malone notched 44 goals and four assists in 1917–18. McDonald scored 66 goals to go with 32 assists for the Flames in 1982–83.

Largest goals-to-assists differential by a defenseman, one season
MODERN-DAY RECORD
12: Adrian Aucoin, Vancouver, 1998–99
11: Sergei Gonchar, Washington, 1998–99
It defies explanation how two defensemen could compile such lopsided differentials, much less in the same season. Aucoin posted 23 goals and 11 assists; Gonchar recorded 21 goals and 10 assists. One thing is clear: both of these guys were sharks on the power play. Aucoin notched 18 of his 23 goals with a man-advantage, while Gonchar counted 13 of 21 on the power play.

Largest assists-to-goals differential by a forward, career
738: Adam Oates, 1985–86 to 2003–04
700: Ron Francis, 1981–82 to 2003–04
We're guessing that neither Oates nor Francis ever had goal-scoring bonuses in their contracts: they were playmakers first and shooters second. Oates topped 200 shots on net only once in 19 seasons (in 1992–93 with Boston, when he scored 45 times). His career numbers are 341 goals and 1,079 assists. Francis reached 200 shots four times in 23 seasons and has registered 549 goals and 1,249 assists.

Largest assists-to-goals differential, one season

111: Wayne Gretzky, Edmonton, 1985–86

81: Wayne Gretzky, Los Angeles, 1990–91

Gretzky's goal production began to slide in 1985–86, but his assists total rose when he amassed 52 goals and 163 assists for a mind-boggling 215 points. Gretzky's second-highest differential was in 1990–91, when he had 41 goals and 122 assists.

Most goalies scored on, career

155: Wayne Gretzky, 1979–80 to 1998–99

Just about every NHL netminder that Gretzky suited up against got skewered.

Most single-season scoring records, career

17: Wayne Gretzky, 1979–80 to 1998–99

Who else? Not only are there a lot of them, few of these records will be easy to break. No. 99's storehouse includes single-season marks for longest consecutive-games scoring streak (51), highest goals-per-game average (1.18), most goals in the first 50 games of the season (61) and most assists in a season, including playoffs (174).

Most games scoring a point, one season

77: Wayne Gretzky, Edmonton, 1985–86

This was a season in which Gretzky made scoring look like child's play, amassing an NHL-record 215 points. There were only three games in which he didn't get on the board: a 2–0 loss to Buffalo in Game 10, a 4–3 win over Chicago in Game 50 and a 7–3 win over Buffalo in Game 69. In 40 of the 80 games on the schedule, Gretzky recorded at least three points; in 21 games, he had four points or more.

Earliest date of a 50th goal by a player, one season
December 30: Wayne Gretzky, Edmonton, 1981

The Edmonton Oilers did something in the 1980s that is considered poor sportsmanship in today's NHL—they ran up the score. During Gretzky's race to become the fastest 50-goal scorer in NHL history, the Oilers mugged opponents with joyful abandon. In an eight-day span in November 1981, Edmonton crushed Vancouver 8–3, Detroit 8–4, Los Angeles 11–4, Chicago 8–1 and Winnipeg 11–2. Gretzky reached the 40-goal plateau in Game 36 against Calgary, got number 41 in the next game against Vancouver, then scored four times in a 10–3 blitz of Los Angeles, giving him 45 in 36 games. On December 30, versus Philadelphia, he hit the mark in spectacular style, putting four pucks past netminder Pete Peeters before depositing his fifth of the game (and his 50th of the season) into an empty net to seal a 7–5 Oilers win.

Highest percentage of power-play goals by a 50-goal scorer, one season

60.8%: Joe Nieuwendyk, Calgary, 1987–88
58.6%: Tim Kerr, Philadelphia, 1985–86

Some guys are absolutely murderous with a man-advantage. A master of the deflection, Nieuwendyk notched 31 of his 51 goals in his rookie season on the Flames' power play in 1987–88. Kerr, who was nicknamed the Human Slot Machine, scored 58 times for the Flyers in 1985–86. Thirty-four of them came with the man-advantage, and most of those came from the slot.

Only player to score his 50th goal of the season on a penalty shot

Mario Lemieux, Pittsburgh, April 11, 1997

Lemieux bagged his sixth 50-goal season in a 1997 game against the Florida Panthers when he scored on a penalty shot at 2:28 of the third period. Goalie John Vanbiesbrouck was the victim, a familiar role for him. It was the 32nd time that Lemieux had beaten the Beezer in his career, which is more goals than even Wayne Gretzky ever scored against a single netminder.

Age of oldest player to score his first 50th goal, one season

35.10 years: Johnny Bucyk, Boston, 1970–71
32.1 years: Joe Mullen, Pittsburgh, 1988–89
31.6 years: Vic Hadfield, NY Rangers, 1971–72

Bucyk played 15 seasons without scoring more than 31 goals, but then in 1970–71, at age 35, he turned on the red light 51 times. The rise in his numbers was a result of playing left wing on Boston's explosive power play. Bucyk connected for 22 power-play goals—only three less than teammate Phil Esposito, who set a new NHL record with 25.

Age of oldest player to record his first 100th point, one season

40.11 years: Gordie Howe, Detroit, 1968–69

We confidently predict this record won't be broken, at least not until scientists start producing bionic hockey players. Mr. Hockey reached the 100-point plateau a day before he turned 41. And although Howe compiled a career-high 103 points in 1968–69, it would be difficult to argue that he was in his prime. After all, this was his 23rd NHL season. Howe's pumped-up performance was aided by expansion and playing a full season on a line with newly acquired left-winger Frank Mahovlich, who combined with centre Alex Delvecchio to offer superstar support.

Earliest date of a 100th point by a player, one season
December 18: Wayne Gretzky, Edmonton, 1983
It took Gretzky only 35 games to reach the century mark in 1983–84, a sizzling pace of nearly three points per game. The Oilers' scoring wizard ended the season with 205 points—double what today's leading scorers rack up.

Most 100-point seasons, career
15: Wayne Gretzky, 1979–80 to 1998–99
For most NHLers, compiling 100 points is a rare achievement. Even Guy Lafleur, Phil Esposito and Steve Yzerman only managed to do it six times. For Gretzky it was just business as usual. He reached the milestone 15 times.

First player to record 100 points in back-to-back seasons with two teams
Mike Rogers, Hartford, 1980–81; NY Rangers, 1981–82
Rogers had just compiled back-to-back 105-point seasons for Hartford when Whalers management, convinced that he wouldn't do it again, traded him to the Rangers for Doug Sulliman, Gerry McDonald and Chris Kotsopolous. The Whalers continued losing and Rogers tailed off—he only scored 103 points for the Rangers.

Fewest goals by a 100-point player, one season
22: Brian Leetch, NY Rangers, 1991–92
23: Adam Oates, St. Louis, 1989–90
23: Wayne Gretzky, Los Angeles and St. Louis, 1995–96
Jumping into the attack at every opportunity, the New York

blueliner racked up 102 points on 22 goals and 80 assists. Maybe the most surprising aspect of Leetch's freewheeling performance in 1991–92, however, was that he did it while playing for defense-first coach Roger Neilson, whom Rangers management would fire a year later for being too conservative. Oates, whose main role with the Blues in 1989–90 was feeding Brett Hull, recorded 102 points on 23 goals and 79 assists. Gretzky posted the same numbers as Oates in a year split between the Kings and the Blues.

Last player to rank among the top-10 scorers with fewer than 10 goals
Bill Gadsby, NY Rangers, 1955–56
Gadsby is one of only a handful of NHLers to rank in the top 10 with fewer than 10 goals, and the only player to achieve the feat in the last 75 years. In 1955–56, the Rangers rearguard compiled 51 points on nine goals and 42 assists to finish ninth in league scoring.

Only player to lead three teams in scoring in consecutive years
Vincent Damphousse, 1990–91, 1991–92, 1992–93
What was it? Bad body odour? In the early 1990s, Damphousse kept getting traded despite a deft touch around the net. In 1990–91, he topped Toronto in scoring with 73 points. But the Leafs promptly dealt him to Edmonton, where he led the Oilers in scoring the next season with 89 points. The Oilers then shipped him to Montreal, where he led the Canadiens in scoring with 97 points.

Only player to outshoot an opposition team, one game
Gordie Howe, Detroit, January 27, 1955
Howe fired 19 shots at Rangers netminder Gump Worsley in a

3–3 tie. Amazingly, he failed to score. Even more amazing was the night's total-shot tally: Detroit, 31, New York, 18. Howe out-shot the entire Rangers team! Another oddity about the game: Gordie's brother, Vic, scored the tying goal for New York. It was the second of just three goals that Vic scored in his NHL career.

Most games played without scoring a goal, career

155: Steve Halko, 1997–98 to 2003–04
120: Dallas Eakins, 1992–93 to 1999–2000
Where is that damn net? In Halko's case, it may as well be in Mongolia. The journeyman defenseman has yet to find the target in 155 games. Eakins probably hopes he never does.

Most power-play goals by a goalie, one season
1: Evgeni Nabokov, San Jose, 2001–02
Do not adjust your set. Nabokov accomplished the hard to imagine when he shot the puck the length of the ice into an empty Vancouver net on March 10, 2002. Down 6–4 with less than a minute to play and a man in the penalty box, the Canucks pulled goalie Peter Skudra and added another attacker in a desperate bid to get a goal. But Nabokov finished them off with his power-play marker.

Most power-play goals by two teammates, one season

55: Mario Lemieux and Rob Brown, Pittsburgh, 1988–89
The Penguins set an NHL record with 119 power-play goals in 1988–89. As you might expect, Lemieux was front and centre in the charge (he led the league with 31 power-play goals), but it's a surprise to see Brown's name. The right-winger enjoyed a career year, scoring 115 points. Twenty-four of Brown's 49 goals came on the power play.

Most points without scoring a point on the power play, one game

8: Maurice Richard, Montreal, December 28, 1944

Every record has a backstory. And the story behind Richard's eight-point night in December 1944 says as much about the record as any in his legendary career. Three days after Christmas, Richard moved his family from their third-floor apartment on Papineau Street in Montreal. Snow covered the outside staircases, but Richard and his brother moved furniture all afternoon to their new digs, a place that afforded his wife, Lucille, one fewer set of stairs to climb. That night he complained of a sore back. But Montreal coach Dick Irvin told him to get ready, he would be playing against Detroit's rookie goalie Harry Lumley. So Richard had a massage, dressed and, in the game, was unstoppable. With both teams at full strength, Richard banged in five goals and assisted on three more, sometimes demonstrating the art of "carrying players on his back" on the way to the net. After the 9–1 whipping, Montreal fans danced in the stands and screamed "Maurice! Maurice!" One sports columnist asked: "Is the Rocket mortal?"

CHAPTER 9

The Boys
on the bus

Looking for an unusual team record

that will be tough to break? Try this

one on for size. From 1960 to 1965, the Punch

Imlach–coached Toronto Maple Leafs went unde-

feated in 159 consecutive games in which they led

after two periods. Opposition comebacks simply

didn't happen. The Leafs' record was 136–0–23 in

that span. You can't shut the door much tighter.

Longest unbeaten streak in home openers

26 years: Montreal Canadiens, 1953–54 to 1979–80

Home sweet home. For an amazing 26 straight seasons, the Canadiens were unbeaten in home openers at the Montreal Forum, with a record of 23–0–3. In the late 1970s, the Habs made a habit of pounding their opponents on opening night. They lambasted Los Angeles 9–0 in 1975; pulverized Pittsburgh 10–1 in 1976 and mangled Minnesota 7–3 in 1977. Montreal's record-setting run finally ended with a 5–4 loss to Chicago on October 11, 1980, a forewarning of the imminent demise of the dynasty team that claimed 15 Stanley Cups in its 26-year span.

Most wins against an opponent, one season
13: Detroit Red Wings vs. Chicago Blackhawks, 1950–51

In the good old days of the Original Six, teams met one another 14 times a season. This was good for creating intense rivalries, but in some cases it also meant intense punishment. In 1950–51, the Red Wings posted 101 points to become the first team in NHL annals to reach the century mark. Chicago finished a distant last with a mere 36 points. The 14 tilts between the two clubs were an ugly spectacle. Detroit won 13 of them and outscored the Hawks 68 to 26.

Most consecutive .500-or-better seasons at home

57: Montreal Canadiens, 1940–41 to 1996–97
38: Chicago Blackhawks, 1958–59 to 1995–96
32: Buffalo Sabres, 1972–73 to 2003–04

Canadiens fans were spoiled. For more than half a century they never had to witness a losing season at home, a streak that began with the appointment of coach Dick Irvin during World War II and lasted until the hiring of Alain Vigneault in 1997–98.

To date, Montreal has had only six losing seasons at home in its 86-year NHL history. Chicago's 38-year run of home-ice supremacy seems to be closely connected with Chicago Stadium. The Hawks have been less impressive since moving into the United Center, posting five losing seasons at home in 10 years. Remarkably, since joining the NHL, the Buffalo Sabres have had only one losing season at home: in 1971–72.

Most consecutive losing seasons at home

8: Colorado Rockies/New Jersey Devils, 1978–79 to 1985–86
7: Boston Bruins, 1960–61 to 1966–67

Even changing cities didn't help. Four of the losing seasons in this record streak were spent in the high-altitude air of Colorado and the other four at sea level in New Jersey. Boston was a horror show until Bobby Orr and Phil Esposito came to town.

Most consecutive .500-or-better seasons on the road

9: Montreal Canadiens, 1957–58 to 1965–66
9: Montreal Canadiens, 1971–72 to 1979–80

The Canadiens were never quite as devastating on the road as they were at the Montreal Forum, but they were still a formidable force during their two major dynasties. The first nine-year streak was set under coach Toe Blake. During the second string, Scotty Bowman was at the helm for eight of the nine years. Montreal's best road record was in 1977–78, when it registered a 27–6–7 mark.

Most consecutive seasons without a winning road record

29: Boston Bruins, 1941–42 to 1969–70
27: Chicago Blackhawks, 1935–36 to 1961–62
26: Minnesota North Stars, 1967–68 to 1992–93

It's a shock to see Boston atop this list, especially when you consider that it had some very good teams during this span, including five Cup finalists and a Cup winner in 1970. Boston turned in its lamest road effort in 1960–61, with a 2–25–8 record.

Largest points disparity between home and road records, one season

38: Buffalo Sabres, 1972–73
36: Chicago Blackhawks, 1983–84
33: Montreal Canadiens, 1953–54

If a team ever deserved to be called homers it is the 1972–73 Sabres. Under coach Joe Crozier, Buffalo was a snappy 30–6–3 at the Auditorium and a listless 7–21–11 on the road, a 38-point differential. In 1983–84, Orval Tessier's Blackhawks folded when forced to play outside Chicago Stadium. Chicago was 25–13–2 at home and 5–29–6 on the road. The split personality of Dick Irvin's Montreal squad in 1953–54 (27–5–3 at home and 8–19–8 on the road) is a mystery, considering the quality of the team. Montreal made it to the Cup finals before losing to Detroit in a seventh-game overtime, on the road.

Largest points disparity between road and home records, one season

15: Florida Panthers, 2002–03
13: New Jersey Devils, 1998–99

Better on the road than at home? It's rare, but it happens. Mike Keenan's Panthers couldn't wait to get out of Miami in 2002–03. They were 8–26–7 at home and 16–19–6 on the road.

Fewest home losses, one season (min. 35 home games)

1: Montreal Canadiens, 1976–77
2: Montreal Canadiens, 1961–62

The Canadiens' lone loss at the Forum came on October 30, 1976, when they were edged 4–3 by Boston. Montreal had trouble with the Bruins during the regular season, dropping three of five meetings with its long-time rival. But it was a different story in the postseason, when Montreal swept Boston in the finals.

Fewest road losses, one season (min. 35 road games)

6: Montreal Canadiens, 1972–73
6: Montreal Canadiens, 1974–75
6: Montreal Canadiens, 1977–78

Do you see a pattern? The Scotty Bowman-coached Montreal teams of the 1970s never lost their competitive edge, even when invading foreign territory. In 1972–73, they were 23–6–10 on the road. In 1974–75, they were 20–6–14. In 1977–78, they were 27–6–7.

Worst home winning percentage, one season

.202: San Jose Sharks, 1992–93
.225: Pittsburgh Penguins, 1983–84

The San Jose Sharks? How about the San Jose Lunch Meat? The real sharks were the suits in NHL headquarters who foisted this excuse for a team on the league in 1992–93. San Jose was a terrible 8–33–1 at home. The Penguins' dismal effort at the Igloo in 1983–84 earned them last place and the bonus of the first pick in the 1984 Entry Draft. They selected Mario Lemieux.

Worst road winning percentage, one season

.024: Ottawa Senators, 1992–93
.025: Washington Capitals, 1974–75

The Senators had an abysmal 1–41–0 mark on the road in their first year. That was a fraction worse than Washington had in its first campaign: the Caps were 1–39–0. Who did these punching bags beat? Ottawa topped the New York Islanders 5–3 on April 10, 1993, in its last road game of the season. And after 37 straight road setbacks, Washington edged the California Seals 5–3 on March 28, 1975, a result that prompted the Caps players to skate joyfully around the empty rink holding aloft an empty garbage can—their version of the Stanley Cup.

Longest home undefeated streak from start of season
25 games: Montreal Canadiens, October 30, 1943 to March 18, 1944

Guess what? There were 25 home games on the Canadiens' schedule and they didn't lose a single one—going 22–0–3. What made Montreal so unbeatable? For one thing, it was Maurice Richard's first full season. The arrival of future Hall of Fame goalie Bill Durnan didn't hurt either. And too, the other teams in the league had lineups stocked with wartime replacement players, a handicap that never severely affected Montreal.

Longest home winless streak
17 games: Ottawa Senators, October 28, 1995 to January 27, 1996
17 games: Atlanta Thrashers, January 19 to March 29, 2000
Ticket refunds were in order in Ottawa and Atlanta. On January 29, 1996, the struggling Senators finally ended their run of ineptitude (15 losses, two ties) by beating St. Louis 4–2. The woeful Thrashers ended their drought (15 losses, two ties) with a 5–4 victory over the Islanders on April 2, 2000.

Longest losing streak that didn't count

18 games: Pittsburgh Penguins, January 13 to February 22, 2004
The Penguins lost 18 straight games in 2003–04, the most by any team in history, but they didn't set a record. That's because one of those losses (to St. Louis) came in overtime, which means it didn't officially count in their total. Yet, according to the NHL, a loss in overtime does count as a defeat if we're talking about an unbeaten streak. In 2003–04, for example, the Toronto Maple Leafs earned points in a franchise-record 16 straight games. But the Leafs' streak wasn't considered an undefeated run because they had one overtime loss (to St. Louis) mixed in. So an overtime loss is not a loss in a losing streak, but it is one in an unbeaten streak. Got that?

Largest one-year increase in goal scoring

122 goals: 277 to 399, Boston Bruins, 1969–70 to 1970–71
112 goals: 242 to 354, Buffalo Sabres, 1973–74 to 1974–75
You might expect this record to belong to a team that had been radically transformed by a trade or by a club whose young players had suddenly blossomed. But the Bruins were the defending Cup champions! Hell-bent on rewriting the record book, Boston boosted its goal total by 122. Phil Esposito scored 76 times, Bobby Orr rang up 102 assists and Johnny Bucyk and Ken Hodge topped 100 points. The Buffalo Sabres' 112-goal hike in 1974–75 can be credited to the return of Gilbert Perreault from an injury and the coming of age of the French Connection Line.

Largest one-year decline in goal scoring

99 goals: 339 to 240, Pittsburgh Penguins, 1975–76 to 1976–77
96 goals: 337 to 241, Toronto Maple Leafs, 1989–90 to 1990–91
With snipers Pierre Larouche, Jean Pronovost and Syl Apps Jr. leading the charge, the Penguins lit up the board in 1976–77. The

next year, under coach Ken Schinkel, the Pens opted for tighter defensive play: Larouche was traded to Montreal and Pittsburgh became a much duller team. Despite the drop in scoring, Pittsburgh finished with only one less point than it had in 1975–76, but the Pens still went belly-up in the playoffs, losing in the first round. In contrast, the Leafs' 96-goal decline in 1990–91 resulted in a 23-point drop in the standings to second-last overall.

Largest one-year increase in goals allowed

109 goals: 199 to 308, Detroit Red Wings, 1969–70 to 1970–71
96 goals: 178 to 274, Chicago Blackhawks, 1945–46 to 1946–47
In Detroit, they say that the Darkness began with Harkness—Ned Harkness, that is. The former Cornell University bench boss, who took over as Red Wings coach and GM in 1970–71, engineered a stunning 40-point freefall in the standings during his first season. Front-office chaos ensued, and the Wings missed the playoffs for seven straight years.

Largest one-year decline in goals allowed

149 goals: 414 to 265, San Jose Sharks, 1992–93 to 1993–94
141 goals: 415 to 274, Detroit Red Wings, 1985–86 to 1986–87
Rookie coach Kevin Constantine convinced the Sharks to pay attention to defense, and goalie Arturs Irbe had a career year. The result was 149 fewer goals allowed and an NHL-record 58-point improvement in the standings. As for the Red Wings, they basically had the same team they had the year before, when they set an NHL record for most goals allowed. What was different in 1986–87 was the coach. Detroit hired Jacques Demers and lowered its goals-against count by 141, resulting in a 38-point jump in the standings.

Largest lead by a division champion, one season

51 points: Montreal Canadiens, 1977–78

49 points: Montreal Canadiens, 1976–77

42 points: Montreal Canadiens, 1975–76

Montreal's dynasty teams in the 1970s had the good fortune
of playing in the weak Norris Division with Los Angeles,
Pittsburgh, Detroit and Washington, an alignment that made
little geographic sense and was never competitive. As a result,
in 1977–78, Montreal amassed 129 points—51 more than the
second-place Red Wings, who finished ninth overall. It was
not until 1981–82 that Montreal moved into the more tightly
contested Adams Division with Boston, Buffalo, Quebec
and Hartford.

Largest gap between last- and second-last-place teams, one season

37 points: Chicago Blackhawks, 1953–54

33 points: Quebec Nordiques, 1989–90

The Blackhawks came perilously close to folding during the 1950s,
when they stumbled to seven last-place finishes in eight years.
But they were at their absolute worst in 1953–54, when they posted
31 points, a whopping 37 behind the fifth-place Rangers. Chicago's
lone bright spot was its shell-shocked netminder, Al Rollins, who
should have been awarded the Purple Heart, but settled for the
Hart Trophy as league MVP.

Last team to lead league in goals for and goals against, one season

Montreal Canadiens, 1977–78

It has been more than 25 years since anyone dominated the NHL like Montreal did in 1977–78. *Les Habitants* scored a league-high 359 goals and allowed a league-low 183. Only two teams since have come close to duplicating the feat. In 1978–79, the New York Islanders led with 358 goals but ranked second in fewest goals allowed with 214, 10 more than Montreal. In 1988–89, the Calgary Flames led with 354 goals and were second in fewest goals allowed, with 226, eight more than the leader, which was— you guessed it—Montreal.

Best power-play scoring percentage, one season (since 1967)
31.9: Montreal Canadiens, 1977–78
31.7: New York Islanders, 1975–76
31.3: New York Islanders, 1977–78
Taking penalties against the 1977–78 Canadiens was like playing Russian roulette with three bullets. Montreal scored 73 power-play goals on 229 chances, a rate of nearly one goal for every three power plays. Steve Shutt scored 16 and Guy Lafleur netted 15. The second-most deadly team in history with the man-advantage was the 1975–76 Islanders—surprisingly, because it was two years before the arrival of sniper Mike Bossy. The Isles' ace was defenseman Denis Potvin, who scored 18 times on the power play, one less than league leader Phil Esposito.

Worst power-play scoring percentage, one season (since 1967)
9.3: Tampa Bay Lightning, 1997–98
9.6: Minnesota Wild, 2000–01
There was no lightning in Tampa Bay's attack. The Bolts scored only 151 goals in 82 games and just 34 on the power play. Mikael Renberg led the team with six. As for the Wild, they scored 37 power-play goals, led by Marion Gaborik with six.

Most consecutive games scoring five goals or more, one season

11: Philadelphia Flyers, October 27 to November 19, 1985

You would suspect that this record would be owned by one of the run-and-shoot Edmonton Oilers teams of the 1980s. But no, it's the property of a Mike Keenan-coached Flyers club. Philly broke out of the gate with a vengeance in 1985–86, taking 15 of its first 17 games, including 13 in a row. The streak overlapped with a string of 11 straight games in which they scored five goals or more. The Flyers' winning streak ended with an 8–6 loss to the Islanders. The streak of scoring five or more goals in a game ended two nights later, when the Flyers beat Hartford 3–0.

Most consecutive games scoring a power-play goal, one season

21: Edmonton Oilers, 1982–83
21: New York Rangers, 1989–90

When you score a power-play goal in 21 straight games, it's a sign that you are firing on all cylinders. Both of these teams could put the puck in the net. Edmonton led the Smythe Division with 106 points and New York led the Patrick Division with 85 points.

Most consecutive playoff years after joining the NHL

13: Edmonton Oilers, 1979–80 to 1991–92

Unlike most expansion clubs, the Oilers were never terrible and quickly became very good. Thanks in large part to a charitable playoff system that qualified 16 of 21 teams, the Oilers were able to slip into the postseason in their first two NHL seasons before suddenly vaulting to the penthouse the next year. After setting its 13-year streak, however, Edmonton missed the postseason for the next four seasons.

Most consecutive seasons missing the playoffs

9: Colorado Rockies/New Jersey Devils 1978–79 to 1986–87

The dangerous Devils of today bear no resemblance to the inept Jersey squads that were stinking up NHL arenas during the franchise's dark years.

Most consecutive regular-season games without being shut out

264: Calgary Flames, November 12, 1981 to January 9, 1985
261: Los Angeles Kings, May 15, 1986 to October 22, 1989

Ah yes, the wonderful high-scoring 1980s. The Flames and Kings both played more than three full seasons without being blanked by an opposition goalie. Calgary's 264-game streak was finally snapped by Quebec Nordiques netminder Richard Sevigny, who goose-egged Calgary 4–0 on January 11, 1985. As it turned out, it was the last shutout of Sevigny's career. The Kings' bid to break Calgary's record was derailed, fittingly, by the Flames, who blanked Los Angeles 5–0 behind the goaltending of Rick Wamsley on October 25, 1989.

Longest span without a shutout against one opponent

37 years: Toronto Maple Leafs vs. NY Rangers, 1966–67 to 2003–04

The last time the Leafs blanked the Rangers was February 15, 1967. Johnny Bower picked up the goose egg in a 6–0 win.

Most consecutive games scoring the first goal

18: Montreal Canadiens, October 18 to November 29, 1959
15: Chicago Blackhawks, December 10, 1967 to January 13, 1968
15: Montreal Canadiens, February 19 to March 18, 1972

No team ever got out of the blocks more quickly than the 1959–60 Habs. In the fifth and final year of their dynasty run, the

Canadiens scored first in 18 straight games. Interestingly, the streak overlapped with Jacques Plante's adoption of a mask on November 1, 1959.

Most consecutive games scoring the first goal from start of season

12: Philadelphia Flyers, October 10 to November 6, 1985
12: Vancouver Canucks, October 9 to November 3, 2003
Does a good start indicate season-long success? The Flyers won a franchise-high 53 games in 1985–86, but lost in the Cup finals. The Canucks' season took an ugly turn with the suspension of Todd Bertuzzi in March, followed by an early playoff exit.

Most consecutive one-goal victories
10: Anaheim Mighty Ducks, January 12 to February 12, 2003

The Mighty Ducks snapped one of the NHL's longest-standing records in February 2003, when they edged Calgary 4–3 for their 10th straight one-goal victory. The previous standard of nine was set by the old Ottawa Senators in 1926–27.

Fewest goals by an expansion team (min. 70 games)
153: Oakland Seals, 1967–68
168: Minnesota Wild, 2000–01
The sickly Seals made other expansion teams look good, winning only 15 games. Despite its pop-gun offense, Minnesota posted 68 points, which was more than four other established NHL teams had in 2000–01.

Most scoring champions

16: Montreal Canadiens
11: Boston Bruins
11: Chicago Blackhawks
11: Pittsburgh Penguins

Although they have not produced a scoring champion in nearly 30 years, the Canadiens remain comfortably ahead in this category. The last Hab to win the scoring derby was Guy Lafleur, in 1977–78. All 11 of Pittsburgh's scoring titles have been won by two players: Mario Lemieux and Jaromir Jagr.

Longest wait for a scoring champion

66 years: Toronto Maple Leafs, 1937–38 to 2003–04
62 years: New York Rangers, 1941–42 to 2003–04

The last time a Toronto player captured the NHL scoring title, Adolph Hilter was just getting started. It's been so long that most Leafs fans can't even name him. For the record, it was Gordie Drillon who, in 1937–38, led the circuit with 26 goals in 48 games. The Rangers' wait has been nearly as long. Their last scoring champion was Bryan Hextall Sr., in 1941–42.

CHAPTER 10

Wheel
of fortune

The first time the first pick in the NHL Entry Draft was decided by the spin of a wheel was in 1970, when the league added two new expansion teams. Vancouver took even numbers and Buffalo took odds. The wheel stopped at 11. The Sabres chose Gilbert Perreault; the Canucks got Dale Tallon. Fate had spoken, and the verdict was unkind to the Canucks.

Most goals by an undrafted player, career (since 1969)

608: Dino Ciccarelli, 1980–81 to 1998–99

Ciccarelli ranks 13th on the all-time goal-scoring chart. Not too shabby for a guy who attracted no interest in the draft. So how did everyone miss Ciccarelli? His junior totals were very marketable. Could it be his mailbox size (five foot ten), or his attitude (one tough wing nut)? The Minnesota North Stars chanced signing Ciccarelli as a free agent and, unlike most young players, he was clearly ready for prime time. In the 1981 playoffs, he pumped in 14 goals and 21 points as the North Stars surged to the Stanley Cup finals. Both numbers remain playoff rookie records. Then, in his second year, he scored 55 goals—five more than in his final year with the OMJHL London Knights.

Most points by an undrafted player, career (since 1969)

1,420: Adam Oates, 1985–86 to 2003–04

Undrafted and unloved. Who knows why 21 NHL teams bypassed Oates in the draft? It's not as if he was a slouch as an amateur. He played three seasons of American college hockey with RPI and led them to the NCAA title in 1984–85. Detroit signed Oates as a free agent in 1985, but then stupidly traded him to St. Louis four years later for an aging Bernie Federko. Oates then proved his worth with the Blues, recording back-to-back 100-point seasons as Brett Hull's set-up man.

Most wins by an undrafted goalie, career (since 1969)

435: Ed Belfour, 1988–89 to 2003–04

Eddie the Eagle slipped under everyone's radar. No NHL team showed any interest in the University of North Dakota goalie in the 1987 Entry Draft. A few months later, Belfour got a tryout with Chicago and was signed as a free agent. In 1991, he was voted the NHL's rookie of the year.

Highest draft pick never to play in the NHL (since 1969)

Ray Martynuik, fifth overall, Montreal, 1970

Martynuik is proof that the Montreal scouts didn't always get it right in the Sam Pollock era. Although the Habs selected the Flin Flon netminder fifth overall, he failed to graduate to the NHL. Worse, Pollock miscued on goaltending gems Billy Smith, Gilles Meloche and Dan Bouchard. It's a good thing the Canadiens' GM had a couple of kids named Ken Dryden and Tony Esposito standing by.

Most NHL games by a last-pick overall (since 1969)

396: Kim Johnsson, 286th, NY Rangers, 1994

Johnsson was the very last pick in the 1984 draft. But the Swede developed into a better player than anyone could have imagined, and the Rangers are probably bummed that they dealt him to Philadelphia in 2001.

Lowest draft pick to play in the NHL

Simon Gamache, 290th, Atlanta, 2000

Gamache had a spectacular final junior season in 2000–01, winning the QMJHL's Jean Béliveau Trophy as leading scorer, the Michel Briere Trophy as MVP and the Guy Lafleur Trophy as playoff MVP. He compiled 74 goals and 110 assists for 184 points in the regular season, then added a record 57 playoff points— erasing the record held by Mario Lemieux. Despite these gaudy numbers, Gamache's lack of size and speed caused NHL scouts to dismiss his chances of making the big time. He debuted with the Thrashers on March 7, 2003, against Florida.

Lowest draft pick to play 500 NHL games

Ken Baumgartner, 245th, Buffalo, 1985

Baumgartner didn't last for 696 NHL games because he could
score—he once went 94 straight games without registering a
point and posted a paltry 54 points in his career. No, the key to
Baumgartner's longevity was his willingness to mix it up. When
he retired in 1999, he had accumulated 2,244 penalty minutes.

Lowest draft pick to win the Calder Trophy

Sergei Makarov, 241st, Calgary, 1983

Makarov was already one of the best players in the world when
Calgary drafted him in 1983. By the time he joined the Flames at
age 31 in 1989, he had won nine scoring titles in the USSR. Then,
in his first NHL campaign, the Russian right-winger recorded 86
points in 80 games to capture the Calder Trophy. But his selection was a controversial one: several teams protested that
Makarov was not truly a rookie. The next year, the NHL changed
its rules governing Calder candidates, lowering the age of eligibility to 26.

Lowest draft pick to score 500 goals

Luc Robitaille, 171st, Los Angeles, 1984

The Kings got lucky in the 1984 draft—Lucky Luc Robitaille,
to be precise. The Montreal-born forward had piled up 191
points in his last season of junior with the Hull Olympiques,
but NHL teams blithely ignored him. At the urging of scout
Alex Smart, the Kings eventually selected Robitaille in the
ninth round, 171st overall, but only after squandering five
straight picks on players who failed to play a single NHL game
(though one of them, Tom Glavine, did have a great career as
a major-league pitcher). Robitaille has scored more goals than
any left-winger in NHL history.

Lowest draft pick to score 100 points, one season

Dave Taylor, 210th, Los Angeles, 1975

Taylor was taken in the final round of the 1975 draft, a desperation pick by the Kings. The Clarkson University grad would go on to play 1,111 NHL games and rack up 1,069 points, more than any other player drafted that year. Taylor also accomplished what no other player in the 1975 draft could—he scored 100 points in a season, and he did it twice, in 1980–81 and 1981–82.

First NHL draft picks, by country of birth

PLAYER	DRAFTED BY	PICK/YEAR	COUNTRY
Garry Monahan	Montreal	1st/1963	Canada
Herb Boxer	Detroit	17th/1968	U.S.A.
Tommi Salmalainen	St. Louis	66th/1969	Finland
Per Alexandersson	Toronto	49th/1974	Sweden
Viktor Khatulev	Philadelphia	160th/1975	Russia
Ladislav Svozil	Detroit	194th/1978	Czechoslovakia
Bernhard Englbrecht	Atlanta	196th/1978	Germany

First high-school player selected in an Entry Draft

Jay North, Buffalo, 1980

NHL teams dipped into the preppy talent pool for the first time in 1980, drafting eight high-schoolers. North, a centre from Bloomington-Jefferson High School in Minnesota, was selected by Buffalo 62nd overall. He never made it to the big time.

First player drafted directly from high school into the NHL

Bobby Carpenter, Washington, 1981

A number of high-profile players were drafted out of high school, including Brian Leetch and Phil Housley, but Carpenter came first, picked third overall by a Washington team hurting for some positive publicity after six straight seasons of missing the playoffs. Carpenter, just 18 years old and fresh out of St. John's High School in Massachusetts, survived his baptism by fire and never looked back.

First goalie drafted directly from high school into the NHL

Tom Barrasso, Buffalo, 1983

Barrasso's feat is remarkable considering that goalies usually require several years of development to reach NHL-calibre play. And not only did Barrasso make the leap to the pros directly from Acton-Boxboro High School in Massachusetts, the 18-year-old captured the Vezina and Calder Trophies and a berth on the First All-Star team.

First goalie drafted directly from junior hockey into the NHL

John Davidson, St. Louis, 1973

After being drafted fifth overall by St. Louis in 1973, the 20-year-old Davidson went from the WCJHL Calgary Centennials to backstopping the Blues in 39 games. The jump in competition didn't seem to bother Davidson, who posted a 3.08 GAA with the Blues, better than his 3.30 GAA in Calgary.

First defenseman drafted first overall (since 1969)

Denis Potvin, NY Islanders, 1973

The 1973 draft had a few up-and-comers, including Lanny McDonald and Bob Gainey, but the sure money was on Potvin, the explosive rushing defenseman who racked up 123 points in 61 games for the junior Ottawa 67s in 1972–73.

First goalie drafted first overall (since 1969)

Rick DiPietro, NY Islanders, 2000

Quick and agile. Great glove. Premier puckhandler. Competitive nature. DiPietro got rave reviews from the scouts, which convinced Isles GM Mike Milbury to take the Boston University freshman first overall in 2000.

First American-born player drafted first overall

Brian Lawton, Minnesota, 1983

Lawton was the can't-miss-kid from Mount St. Charles High School who never fulfilled the enormous expectations of a first-overall pick. The North Stars passed on Pat LaFontaine, Steve Yzerman, Cam Neely, Tom Barrasso, Russ Courtnall and John MacLean, who all went in the top 10 that year.

First U.S. college player drafted first overall

Joe Murphy, Detroit, 1986

Born in London, Ontario, Murphy was among a growing number of players who chose college over the Canadian junior leagues during the 1980s. After recording 61 points in 35 games with Michigan State in 1985–86, the Spartans' flashy right-winger was selected first overall by Detroit.

First European-trained player drafted first overall

Mats Sundin, Quebec, 1989

The 1989 Entry Draft wasn't a banner year for North American prospects, but there were several hotshots lurking in Europe (Sergei Fedorov, Pavel Bure, Nicklas Lidstrom and Bobby Holik). Picking first overall, the Nordiques took the Swedish centre with the broad wingspan.

First Russian-trained player drafted first overall
Ilya Kovalchuk, Atlanta, 2001

A decade after the first Russians began trickling into the NHL, the biggest star-in-waiting was a kid from Tver, Russia. Kovalchuk was selfish with the puck, rebellious and headstrong, but he was also the best prospect in 2001, and that's why the Thrashers made him number one.

Most rebellious first-overall draft pick

Eric Lindros, Quebec, 1991

Lindros shook up the hockey world by declaring he would not play for the Nordiques if they drafted him with their first pick in 1991, claiming that he didn't want to play in a backwater like Quebec City. The Nords drafted him anyway, but Lindros refused to budge, becoming a figure of derision in the province of Quebec. A year later, Quebec traded Lindros to Philadelphia for a package of six players, including Peter Forsberg.

Only first-overall draft pick on a Stanley Cup winner in rookie season

Réjean Houle, Montreal, 1971

Because bad teams get the first pick and because number one

draft picks on bad teams usually quickly graduate to the NHL, the odds are stacked against them playing for a Cup winner as a rookie. Montreal, which did not have a bad team, utilized its territorial perogative to nab Houle in 1969. But he played only nine games with the Habs in 1969–70, thus preserving his rookie status, before becoming a full-time player the next season. Although Houle was overshadowed by rookie goalie Ken Dryden in the 1971 playoffs, he acquitted himself admirably, playing in all 20 of Montreal's postseason games and recording seven points.

Only first-round draft pick to lead NHL in penalties
Jimmy Mann, Winnipeg, 1979
Anyone who thinks the hiring of John Ferguson as Winnipeg's GM was a clever move need look no further than his first major decision as an NHL hockey boss. With the expansion Jets' first pick (19th overall) in the 1979 Entry Draft, Fergie chose tough guy Jimmy Mann from the Quebec Junior League's Sherbrooke Beavers. The pugnacious rookie proved he could fight, topping the NHL with 287 PIM in 1979–80. He also proved that he couldn't score (he netted just three goals and a total of 10 over his entire career). Who could Ferguson have picked instead? Let's see: Mark Messier, Michel Goulet, Glenn Anderson, Dale Hunter, Guy Carbonneau and Kevin Lowe, to name but a few.

Only player drafted after already playing two NHL seasons
Don McLeod, Pittsburgh, 1973
McLeod doesn't occupy much real estate in the NHL record books, but this oddity is his alone. After playing 18 games in two seasons with Detroit and Philadelphia, he found himself selected 164th overall by Pittsburgh in 1973. How did it happen? We're not sure. By this point, McLeod had already jumped to the WHA, where he played six years, twice leading the league in wins.

First twins drafted

Patrik and Peter Sundstrom, 1980 and 1981

One of six sets of twins drafted to date, the Sundstroms are
the only twins not chosen in the same year. Patrik was selected
175th by Vancouver in 1980, while Peter was taken 50th by the
Rangers in 1981.

Most hotly contested draft pick

Pavel Bure, Vancouver, 1989

Vancouver's selection of Bure in the sixth round of the 1989
Entry Draft caused a major ruckus at the Met Center in Bloom-
ington, Minneapolis. Representatives from several teams raced
to the head table to vehemently protest—hurling expletives at
the Canuck brass. At dispute was Bure's eligibility. Most teams
felt the winger had not played enough elite level games in Russia
to qualify for the draft. Washington and Hartford subsequently
filed complaints with the league, and NHL president John Ziegler
eventually ruled in their favour and disqualified Bure. However,
on the eve of the 1980 draft, the Canucks presented new
evidence to support their case and Ziegler reversed his position,
allowing the Canucks' pick to stand.

Most sons of NHL players drafted in first round, one year

4: 2003

How far does the apple fall from the tree? A record four former
NHLers saw their sons taken in the first round of 2003. Kent
Nilsson's son, Robert, was picked 15th by the New York Islanders;
J.P. Parise's son, Zach, 17th by New Jersey; Steve Tambellini's
son, Jeff, 27th by Los Angeles, and Mike Eaves's son, Patrick,
29th by Ottawa. The crop looks good: Nilsson broke Markus
Naslund's Swedish Elite League record for most points by a
17-year-old; Parise was a 2003 Hobey Baker finalist for North

Dakota; Tambellini led the University of Michigan in scoring as a rookie in 2002–03; Eaves is a graduate of the U.S. National Team Development Program.

Most players drafted, one year

293: 2000

Not considered a big-name year with no clear-cut choice for number one, the 2000 Entry Draft made draft history when the New York Islanders picked Rick DiPietro, the first goalie to go first overall; and St. Louis chose unknown Finnish rearguard Lauri Kinos, the last pick in the ninth round, 293rd overall. Even though each draft year has only nine rounds, some years see more players selected because teams get compensatory picks for their unsigned players who re-enter the draft.

Most players drafted out of high school, one year
69: 1987

Almost 28 per cent of the players selected at the 1987 Entry Draft came from U.S. high schools and prep schools. Although most of the record 69 high-schoolers went in the late rounds and never played an NHL game, there were exceptions, including Joe Sacco, chosen 71st overall, Ted Donato, 98th and Shawn McEachern, 110th. Each has played more than 700 career games.

Most goalies drafted, one year

36: 1993

Typically, about 20 goalies are selected each draft, but in 1993 that total nearly doubled. Despite the year's big run on netminders, however, only four from the 1993 lottery have become NHL regulars: Jocelyn Thibault, selected 10th by the Nordiques, Kevin

Weekes, picked 41st by Florida, Tommy Salo, taken 118th by the Islanders and Patrick Lalime, picked 156th by Pittsburgh.

Most goalies drafted by a team, one year

7: Montreal Canadiens, 1977

Although Montreal already had the Vezina Trophy-winning duo of Ken Dryden and Bunny Larocque in the nets in 1977, the club decided to deepen its talent pool. Montreal selected goalies Robbie Holland, Richard Sevigny, Barry Borrett, Mark Holden, Carey Walker, Jean Belisle and Bob Daly. But only Sevigny became an NHL regular.

Only team to draft an imaginary player

Buffalo Sabres, 1974

Who says Punch Imlach had no sense of humour? At the 1974 draft, the Sabres GM selected Tara Tsujimoto from the Tokyo Kanatas of the Japanese League with his club's second-last pick, 183rd overall. No one had ever heard of Tsujimoto—with good reason. He did not exist. Imlach had plucked the name from the Buffalo telephone book. "I just wanted to add a little fun to those dreary proceedings," Imlach explained.

Most first-round draft picks traded by a team in return for only one player

3: Hartford Whalers, 1995

In a fit of panic, Whalers GM Jim Rutherford risked his team's future, acquiring less-than-spectacular defenseman Glen Wesley from the Boston Bruins in exchange for first-round picks in three straight drafts: 1995, 1996 and 1997. Boston used the picks to draft Kyle McLaren, Jonathan Aitken and Sergei Samsonov.

First team to forfeit its first-round draft pick to sign a coach

New York Rangers, 1978

After four straight losing seasons, New York tried to change its fortunes by luring Fred Shero away from the Philadelphia Flyers and appointing him GM and coach. As a penalty for signing Shero, who still had a year remaining on his contract, New York had to forfeit its first-round draft pick in 1978 to the Flyers, who used the pick to draft Ken Linseman. Under Shero, the Rangers improved by 18 points and upset Philadelphia in the semifinals before falling to Montreal in the finals. Shero never got the Rangers that close again and was fired two years later.

First team to build a dynasty at two consecutive drafts

Edmonton Oilers, 1979 and 1980

The NHL made it tough for Edmonton, Winnipeg, Hartford and Quebec (the four former WHA teams) when the two leagues merged in 1979. Even though they were expansion teams, they were given the last four seeds in the 21-team draft. But the Oilers defied the odds. Due to a technicality, they were able to reclaim Wayne Gretzky as an underage junior prior to the 1979 draft. From this promising start, they proceeded to take Kevin Lowe, 21st overall, Mark Messier, 48th and Glenn Anderson, 69th. The following year, the Oilers snapped up Paul Coffey, sixth overall, Jari Kurri, 69th and Andy Moog, 132nd. All seven players would play integral roles in Edmonton's 1980s dynasty.

Only team forced to skip the draft
St. Louis Blues, 1983

After the NHL blocked the sale of the financially troubled Blues to a Saskatoon group, the club's owner, Ralston Purina, put padlocks on the doors of the Checkerdome and began the process of liquidating the franchise. As a result, the Blues did not participate in the 1983 Entry Draft. The league assumed control of the team and kept it in St. Louis by selling it to entrepreneur Harry Ornest for a bargain-basement price of US$3 million.

Last team to enjoy a "cultural option" in the draft
Montreal Canadiens, 1969

When the original Amateur Draft began in 1963, the Canadiens were granted the option of selecting up to two players of French heritage before any other team could make its first pick. Montreal exercised the clause in 1969 to pick Rejean Houle and Marc Tardif, two of the best talents available that year. After the 1969 draft, the NHL ruled that the Canadiens could not exercise the cultural option again unless all other GMs agreed to reinstate it. That effectively killed it. In 1970, under the new rules, the Buffalo Sabres picked first and chose French star Gilbert Perreault.

CHAPTER 11

Behind
the bench

The life of an NHL coach is never secure. Pat Burns won the Jack Adams Award as coach of the year three times with a record three different teams. Each of those teams also gave him the boot. After winning the award first time with Montreal in 1989, Burns joked: "I didn't want to be coach of the year, I only wanted to be coach for a year."

Most tragic start to a coaching career

Bernie Geoffrion, NY Rangers, 1968–69

As omens go, this was a bad one. In the first hour of Geoffrion's first workout session at the Rangers' 1968 training camp, 29-year-old journeyman Wayne Larkin collapsed during a skating drill. It soon became apparent that he was in serious trouble. Geoffrion jumped over the boards, climbed on top of the stricken player and began pumping his chest, but to no avail. Larkin died of a massive heart attack. Geoffrion's job behind the bench ended mid-January, when he was relieved of his duties because of stress.

Most bizarre conditioning edict by a coach

Car driving, Leo Dandurand, Montreal, 1920–21

Hockey coaches can be a superstitious bunch, especially when things aren't going well. During the 1920–21 season, for example, Dandurand banned his players from driving. The Canadiens coach was convinced that all the time his players were spending in their fancy motor cars was causing their arm and leg muscles to cramp up.

Most wins by a coach fired midseason

41: Robbie Ftorek, New Jersey, 1999–2000

A few other coaches have won more games in a full season and then been cut loose after their clubs flopped in the playoffs, but Ftorek's case is unique. He was canned with eight games left in the 1999–2000 season and his team 16 games above .500. GM Lou Lamoriello explained that he didn't think the Devils could win the Cup with Ftorek. We'll never know. New Jersey went on to win the Cup that year with Ftorek's late-season replacement, Larry Robinson.

Fastest firing of a coach from the start of a season
I game: Paul Thompson, Chicago, 1944–45

It was a quick good-bye. After 14 seasons with Chicago, eight as a player and six as a coach, Thompson was sent packing after the first game of the 1944–45 season, an 11–5 loss to Toronto. He was replaced by Johnny Gottselig.

Fewest games remaining when a coach was fired, one season
2: Michel Bergeron, NY Rangers, 1988–89

Rangers GM Phil Esposito gave up a first-round draft pick and US$100,000 to procure Bergeron from the Quebec Nordiques, but the honeymoon was brief. The two men came to hate one another (probably because they were so similar), and Esposito fired Bergeron with just two games left in the 1988–89 season and the Rangers in a playoff race. He then took over behind the bench, claiming he had sacked Bergeron for insubordination. Bergeron insisted that Esposito just wanted to steal the glory by staging a postseason run. If that was the plan, it didn't work. The Rangers lost their last two games and were swept by Pittsburgh in the first round of the playoffs.

Only coach to fire himself, twice
Mike Milbury, NY Islanders, January 27, 1997 and January 21, 1999

Since becoming the Islanders' GM in December 1995, Milbury has hired and fired eight coaches. Mad Mike even gave himself the boot—not once, but twice. The first time was in January 1997, when he stepped down after a meeting with the Isles brass. As he told reporters, "In some ways I wanted to have the whole enchilada. I gave it up reluctantly." A year later, Milbury axed Rick Bowness and reclaimed his spot behind the bench. But

45 games into the 1998–99 season, with the Isles floundering, Milbury once again removed himself and made Bill Stewart head coach. "It's obvious things didn't go very well, and when things don't go well, changes have to be made," said Milbury. What didn't change was Milbury's status as GM. He somehow retained his job, even though his team missed the playoffs in each of his first six years on Long Island.

Only Cup-winning coach to start the next season in the minors
Al MacNeil, Montreal to Halifax, 1971

After replacing Claude Ruel midway through the 1970–71 season, MacNeil directed Montreal to playoff upsets over Boston and Chicago and won the Cup. But along the way, the rookie coach clashed with several of his stars over ice time, including Henri Richard, who, after Game 5 of the Cup finals, called MacNeil "the worst coach I've ever played for." The Quebec media jumped all over the story, and MacNeil even received death threats. Two weeks after Montreal's Cup parade, GM Sam Pollock told Mac-Neil that he would not be coming back and offered him a job coaching the Canadiens' AHL team in Halifax. Surprisingly, Mac-Neil accepted. Pollock then hired coach Scotty Bowman, who won five Cups in the next eight years. MacNeil spent those eight years patiently running the show in Halifax until Bowman's exit in 1979, when Montreal snubbed him again and named Bernie Geoffrion head coach.

First pro hockey coach to assault a team mascot
Don Jackson, Cincinnati Cyclones, February 4, 1995

Atlanta Knights mascot Sir Slapshot thought it would be amusing to charge down the aisle and slam into the Plexiglas behind the visiting Cincinnati Cyclones bench. What Sir Slapshot didn't know was that the glass was the only thing supporting crippled

Cyclones coach Don Jackson, who had just rejoined the club after suffering multiple leg fractures in a car accident. Jackson was sent sprawling, but he got up, scaled the glass divider and began furiously pummelling Sir Slapshot's inflated head with both fists. Jackson received a 10-game suspension and US$1,000 fine, while the man inside the mascot costume, 26-year-old Mike Centanni, became an overnight Atlanta celebrity.

First NHL coach to assault a team mascot
Craig MacTavish, Edmonton, January 20, 2003

It was a case of the tongue wagging the coach. After being taunted by Calgary Flames mascot Harvey the Hound during a game in 2002–03, MacTavish grabbed Harvey's dangling red tongue, tore it out of his mouth and tossed it into the crowd. When the tongueless Harvey continued to goad MacTavish, the Oilers coach threatened him with a stick. Said MacTavish later: "Most people think I should have put it (the tongue) in my pocket like a handkerchief, but I wasn't thinking that rationally at the time."

Only coach whose name is synonymous with misspeaking
Jean Perron, 1985–86 to 1988–89

Baseball has its "Berraisms," hockey its "Perronisms." The former Canadiens/Nordiques coach-turned-broadcaster is infamous in Quebec for his verbal gaffes. "Ron Hextall's only weakness is between his legs"; "This type of injury is very painful, especially when it hurts"; "We're finally starting to see the train at the end of the tunnel." Funny as he is, Perron does not have much of a sense of humour, however. He filed a $60,000 lawsuit after two writers published a book entitled *Les Perronisms,* a satirical look at Perron's on-air bloopers. (A judge tossed the suit out of court.)

First coach suspended for signing a contract with a rival team

Pat Quinn, Los Angeles, 1986–87

On December 24, 1986, while he was still coaching the Los Angeles Kings, Quinn secretly signed a contract to coach the Vancouver Canucks. When news of the pact leaked to the media, NHL president John Ziegler demanded that Canucks owner Frank Griffiths rip up the contract. Griffiths refused and Ziegler expelled Quinn from the league for "dishonourable conduct," then fined the Canucks US$310,000—$10,000 a day for each day that Quinn had continued to coach the Kings after coming to terms with Vancouver. A subsequent NHL investigation led to Quinn's reinstatment in May 1987, but he was still banned from coaching for three years. The Canucks' fine was later reduced to US$10,000.

Last coach to earn more money than any player on his team

Dick Irvin, Chicago, 1955–56

When Irvin was hired to coach the Chicago Blackhawks in 1955, owner James Norris gave him a contract worth $20,000 a year. That was more than any player on the team was making.

Most games coached without getting official credit

32: King Clancy, Toronto

Clancy, who was a fixture in the Maple Leafs' front office for decades, often stepped into the breach when one of Toronto's coaches was sidelined with illness. He is known to have coached 30 games—10 in relief of Punch Imlach in 1966–67 and 20 in relief of John McLellan in 1971–72 (including five playoff games) for a 17–8–5 record. However, the NHL mysteriously credits all those games to the coaching records of Imlach and McLellan.

Longest span between coaching jobs
21 years: John Muckler, 1968–69 to 1989–90
21 years: Al MacNeil, 1981–82 to 2002–03
Muckler coached the Minnesota North Stars for 35 games in 1968–69, then vanished into the minors. He resurfaced in the NHL two decades later with the Edmonton Oilers and coached the club to the Cup in 1990. MacNeil, who had last coached with Calgary in 1981–82, had a brief 11-game stay behind the Flames bench at age 67, in 2002–03, serving as a replacement for fired coach Greg Gilbert.

Longest span between coaching jobs with the same team
24 years: Dick Irvin, Chicago
Irvin began his storied coaching career in Chicago in 1928–29. He left after the 1930–31 season and moved on to coach the Maple Leafs and the Canadiens. Twenty-four years later, he returned to the Windy City to guide the Blackhawks to last place in 1955–56. Irvin retired after the season because of failing health.

Age of oldest coach
69.1 years: King Clancy, Toronto, 1971–72
68.9 years: Scotty Bowman, 2001–02
Officially, the record holder is Scotty Bowman at 68 years, nine months, but unofficially it's Clancy, who was 69 years, one month when he took over the Leafs' helm in the 1972 playoffs after head coach John McLellan was sidelined with a duodenal ulcer. However, the NHL doesn't credit Clancy with coaching those games.

Age of oldest rookie coach

59.2 years: Bill Dineen, Philadelphia, 1991–92

Dineen had three sons who made it into the NHL before he did. But at 59 years, two months, Dineen finally got his first taste of the big leagues when he was hired by the Flyers in midseason to replace Paul Holmgren.

Most winning seasons

28: Scotty Bowman, 1966–67 to 2001–02
19: Dick Irvin, 1928–29 to 1955–56

Here's more evidence of why Bowman is considered the best bench boss of all time. He had only two losing seasons in his 30-year career, both with Buffalo, in 1985–86 and 1986–87.

Most losing seasons

10: Sid Abel, 1952–53 to 1975–76
10: Milt Schmidt, 1954–55 to 1975–76
9: Jack Adams, 1927–28 to 1946–47

Abel and Schmidt were more successful as players than they were as bench jockeys. Adams would hold this record but for the fact that Abel and Schmidt each spent portions of two losing seasons subbing as interim coaches on expansion teams.

Best coaching record in first 100 games

72–19–9: Tom Johnson, Boston, 1970–71 to 1971–72

Johnson moved behind Boston's bench at an opportune time. In 1970–71, Bobby Orr and company set a new NHL record for goals (399) and wins (57). Although Boston didn't claim the Cup for its rookie coach, it did take care of business in Johnson's second year, a season in which the club compiled 54 wins.

Fewest games to record 300 wins
525: Toe Blake, Montreal, October 6, 1955 to January 3, 1963
528: Glen Sather, Edmonton, October 10, 1979 to March 5, 1986

Blake reached the 300-win plateau in his eighth season. His Canadiens posted four first-place finishes and won five Cups in his first five seasons as bench boss. Sather made a run at Blake's record with the Oilers in the 1980s, but came up three games short. Blake's record was 300–133–92; Sather's was 300–155–73.

Worst winning percentage, career (min. 200 games)
.285: Curt Fraser, 1999–2000 to 2002–03
.341: Fred Glover, 1968–69 to 1973–74
.352: Tom McVie, 1975–76 to 1991–92

Unsuccessful coaches usually don't stick around for long. But Fraser managed to survive 279 games with the Atlanta Thrashers before getting turfed midway through his fourth season. His record was an abysmal 64–184–31.

Longest streak of undefeated games from start of career
10: Dave Gill, Ottawa, 1926–27

Gill, who had been the Senators' GM, added the coaching job to his portfolio after first-place Ottawa failed to perform up to expectations in the 1926 playoffs. The rookie coach got off to a fast start, posting a 9–0–1 record in his first 10 games. The streak ended when the Senators were beaten 5–0 by the league's worst team, the Detroit Cougars, on December 16, 1926. But Ottawa regained its momentum and went on to win the Cup.

Longest unbeaten streak, one season
35 games: Pat Quinn, Philadelphia, 1979–80

Quinn was calling the shots when the Philadelphia Flyers went unbeaten in 35 consecutive games in 1979–80, the longest streak by a team in the history of North American pro sports. As you might guess, Quinn was voted NHL coach of the year. The following year he was rewarded with a five-year contract. A year later, with his injury-riddled club in a slump, Quinn was fired.

Longest winless streak from start of career
9 games: Tom McVie, Washington, 1975–76
9 games: Mike Smith, Winnipeg, 1980–81

McVie began his NHL career in a difficult place—behind the bench of the second-year Capitals. He went 0–8–1 in his first nine games before his struggling club beat Chicago 7–5. Smith was the third coach employed by the hapless Jets in their second NHL season. He went 0–7–2 in his first nine games before his team upset Montreal 4–2. Smith posted only one more win with Winnipeg in 23 games. This stint ended his NHL coaching career.

Longest winless streak from start of season
15 games: Frank Boucher, NY Rangers, 1943–44

Boucher's fifth year behind the Rangers' bench was a nightmare from start to finish. With a roster depleted by World War II call-ups, the Blueshirts began the season with an NHL record 11 straight losses. New York finally posted its first win in its 16th game against Boston on December 12, 1943, thanks to the inspirational play of goalie Ken McAuley. With three minutes left in the second period and the score tied 3–3, the rookie took a puck in the mouth and had to leave for repairs. The three remaining minutes were added to the third period, in which the bloodied McAuley played spectacularly and the Rangers scored three times for a 6–4 victory.

Longest winless streak, one season
25 games: Tom McVie, Winnipeg, 1980–81
The second stop in McVie's NHL coaching career proved as hellish as his first with Washington. After winning the third game of the 1980–81 season, his lifeless Jets went without a victory for 25 consecutive games. With a 1–20–7 record, McVie was handed his pink slip and replaced by Bill Sutherland.

Largest points increase with one team in back-to-back seasons
40: Harry Sinden, Boston, 1966–67 to 1967–68
33: Dick Irvin, Montreal, 1942–43 to 1943–44
32: Al Arbour, NY Islanders, 1973–74 to 1974–75
What a difference a trade can make. The Bruins acquired Phil Esposito, Ken Hodge and Fred Stanfield from Chicago and rocketed from 44 to 84 points. GM Milt Schmidt engineered the heist, but it was 35-year-old Sinden, in his second season as Boston's coach, who ended up looking like a magician.

Largest points increase with two teams in back-to-back seasons
26: Brian Sutter, St. Louis to Boston, 1991–92 to 1992–93
After an 83-point season with St. Louis in 1991–92, Sutter was dumped by the Blues because his club couldn't get past Chicago in the playoffs. He found employment the next season in Boston, where he boosted the Bruins from 84 to 109 points. Despite winning the Adams Division, however, Sutter's Bruins were swept by Buffalo in the opening round of the playoffs.

Largest points decline with one team in back-to-back seasons

38: Sid Abel, Chicago, 1952–53 to 1953–54
37: Scotty Bowman, Detroit, 1995–96 to 1996–97
36: Orval Tessier, Chicago, 1982–83 to 1983–84

No coach has endured such a steep drop in the standings as Abel did with Chicago in 1953–54. The Hawks dive-bombed from 69 to 31 points and missed the playoffs by 38 points. As you might suspect, it cost Abel his job. Bowman's Red Wings slumped from 131 to 94 points, but no one was calling for his head after Detroit captured the Cup.

Largest points decline with two teams in back-to-back seasons

72: Bep Guidolin, Boston to Kansas City, 1973–74 to 1974–75
60: Rick Bowness, Boston to Ottawa, 1991–92 to 1992–93

Lured by a larger contract, Guidolin left the first-place Boston Bruins—after steering them to a 113-point season in 1973–74—to take the head coaching job with the expansion Kansas City Scouts. Instead of Bobby Orr, his best player was now Simon Nolet. Forced to begin the season with a nine-game road trip (because the team's arena was occupied by a rodeo and livestock show), K.C. went winless in its first nine games. Midway through the year, Guidolin was asked if he was having nightmares coaching the Scouts. "You gotta sleep before you have nightmares," he replied. The Scouts posted 41 points, second worst in the NHL, and Guidolin was fired 45 games into his second season. Even worse, he failed to collect on the money owed to him when the franchise folded at the end of the year.

CHAPTER 12

You Can
quote me

Can a quote be a record? In this book it can. For example: Most revealing glimpse inside the mind of a hockey thug. "I'd rather fight than score. Scoring is over in a second, but a good fight can last awhile and you've got time to enjoy it." The source of the quote was former Philadelphia Flyers enforcer Dave "the Hammer" Schultz, who racked up a monstrous 472 penalty minutes in 1974–75.

Most famous hockey phrase
"He shoots, he scores!"
Foster Hewitt, February 16, 1923

Hewitt coined the phrase during his first broadcast of a 1923
senior hockey game, and it's been a standard in play-by-play
ever since. Interestingly, new research has revealed that, contrary
to Hewitt's recollection in his 1967 autobiography, the game actually
occurred five weeks earlier than the previously accepted date of
March 22, 1923.

Best remembered hockey quote in America

"Do you believe in miracles?"
Al Michaels, ABC Sports, 1980 Winter Olympics
Sports Illustrated's choice for its number one 20th-century
moment in sports was the victory by the U.S.A.'s Miracle
on Ice team, which upset the highly favoured Soviet squad
4–3 to advance to the gold-medal game against Finland.
Michael's famous call still reverberates through the pantheon
of American sports.

Most famous quote about what it takes to win

"If you can't beat them in the alley, you can't beat them on the ice."
Conn Smythe, Toronto GM, 1930s
One of hockey's most belligerent characters, Smythe knew
how to win, and that meant playing hard-knuckled hockey.
Smythe guided the Maple Leafs to seven Stanley Cups during
his 29 years as GM.

Most mathematically precise description of winning hockey psychology

"Half the game is mental. The other half is being mental."
Jim McKenny, Toronto, 1970s
The free-spirited McKenny could often be counted on for a loopy quip.

Simplest scouting philosophy

"If they can fit through the door, I don't want 'em."
Milt Schmidt, Boston GM, 1960s
The architect behind the Big Bad Bruins, Schmidt was a graduate of the old school of slam-bam hockey.

Most confused appeal to family values

"We have to get families back in the game, get back where Saturday night, everything stops. A case of beer comes out and a bottle of rye and anyone who comes to the house, they better want to watch hockey."
Bobby Hull, 2004
Many people believe hockey has lost something. Hull evidently thinks it is getting smashed in front of the tube. The new World Hockey Association commissioner was trying to publicize the rebirth of the former league, slated to begin play in fall 2004.

Most convincing argument for wearing a protective cup, but not a helmet

"You can always hire someone to think for you, but . . ."
Gordie Howe, Detroit, 1960s
Howe had a point.

Best reason for deciding to wear a helmet

"I want to spend my summers cutting grass rather than pushing up daisies."
Stan Mikita, Chicago, 1969

Mikita was one of the first NHLers to voluntarily don a helmet after Minnesota North Stars forward Bill Masterton died when his skull was fractured in a game on January 13, 1968.

Worst grasp of nutritional requirements

"Bud Light."
Keith Tkachuk, St. Louis, 2002

This was Tkachuk's response when asked by the St. Louis Blues Media Guide to name his favourite sports drink.

Most virile pre-game ritual

"My pre-game meal on the road is a steak and a blonde."
Derek Sanderson, Boston, 1970s

Sanderson lived a fast life off-ice—too fast, as it turned out. The 1968 rookie of the year never fulfilled his enormous hockey promise.

Most comical observation on adjusting to life in the minors

"One road trip we were stuck on the runway for seven hours. The plane kept driving and driving until we arrived at the rink, and I realized we were on a bus."
Glenn Healy, Toronto, 1999

After 12 seasons in the NHL, Healy woke up to find himself tending net in 1999 with the Chicago Wolves of the IHL.

Most mysterious quote by a rookie goalie

"I was talking to my goalposts."
Patrick Roy, Montreal, May 5, 1986

After a dramatic overtime win in Game 3 of the 1986 Conference finals, Roy was asked by New York reporters why he stared at his net after the national anthem. The rookie netminder responded, in broken English, that he was talking to his posts. The New York scribes loved the quote. Later, when his English improved, Roy explained that he really doesn't speak to his posts, he simply creates a vision of the nets getting smaller.

Most masochistic explanation for choosing to be a goalie

"I just made up my mind I was going to lose teeth and have my face cut to pieces. It was easy."
Johnny Bower, Toronto, 1960s

Before the advent of the mask, goalkeepers paid regular visits to arena clinics. Bower spent more than a few minutes under the needle. By the end of his career, his face was a road map of wear and tear.

Best explanation for being close-shaven

"I stitch better when my skin is smooth."
Lorne Chabot, Toronto goalie, 1930s

Chabot's reply as to why he always shaved before games speaks volumes about the perils of the maskless goaltending era.

Best answer to a dumb question

"Yeah, the two that went in."
Gerry Cheevers, Boston goalie, December 4, 1979

After a 2–2 tie against the Philadelphia Flyers, Cheevers was asked by a reporter if he recalled any shots that were particularly difficult to handle.

Most sobering assessment of coaching as a career option

"Coaching is like being a king. It prepares you for nothing."
Herb Brooks, Olympic and NHL coach, 1990s
Brooks, who led the U.S. Olympic team to its miracle victory in 1980, posted a 219–222–66 record as an NHL bench boss.

Best analysis of a last-place coach's dilemma

"I have four guys who don't understand a word I'm saying, 10 guys who do understand but don't do a thing I tell them to do, and another four who aren't good enough to do what I tell them to do."
Tom McVie, New Jersey, 1983–84
McVie had the dubious pleasure of coaching the Devils during a season in which the club set a franchise record of 56 losses.

Most amusing depiction of coaching frustration

"Last season we couldn't win at home, and this season we can't win on the road. My failure as a coach is that I can't think of any place else to play."
Harry Neale, Vancouver, 1980–81
If Neale was as good at coaching as he was at delivering one-liners, he would rival Scotty Bowman in Stanley Cup rings. Neale used humour to alleviate depression while running the Canucks, a 142–189–76 team under his five-year tutelage.

Most childish insult directed at a referee by a coach

"Have another donut, you fat pig!"
Jim Schoenfeld, New Jersey, May 6, 1988
After his Devils were trounced 6–1 by Boston during the 1988

Conference finals, Schoenfeld confronted referee Don Koharski in a hallway beneath Brendan Byrne Arena and raged over the officiating. As the chubby Koharski walked away, Schoenfeld let loose, his vitriol captured by TV cameras. The irate coach was suspended for one game.

Most backhanded compliment about another coach

"Mike Keenan has been responsible for creating a lot of good things for coaches, like midseason job openings."
Marc Crawford, Vancouver, 1999

As a number of coaches had before him, Crawford found NHL employment after Keenan was given the heave-ho. In this case, by the Canucks—45 games into the 1998–99 campaign.

Most puzzling compliment by a coach

"He has a great body for a hockey player. I don't want this to come out the wrong way, but he has a really nice rear end."
Paul Holmgren, Hartford coach, 1995

We're not sure how this quote could come out any way but wrong. Holmgren was describing the shapely derriere of Whalers forward Andrei Nikolishin.

Most cold-blooded view of a coach by one of his own players

"I would be sitting there thinking about Keenan and how I wanted to kill him. In my mind, I'd be cutting his eyes out with my stick."
Brett Hull, St. Louis, 1995–96

Obviously, Hull wasn't a member of the Mike Keenan fan club. When Iron Mike ran the Blues in 1995–96, he stripped Hull of his captaincy and regularly tore ragged strips off his top scorer's hide. But in the end, the Golden Brett got the last laugh. Keenan was fired the following season, while Hull remained in Missouri.

Best explanation of why head games were futile against the Philadelphia Flyers in the 1970s

"They always try to play with our minds. But that won't work with our club. We have 20 guys without brains."
Bobby Clarke, Philadelphia, 1976
It's tough to tell if Clarke was kidding. The rampaging Flyers often played like they were several cards short of a full deck.

Most grammatically incorrect game summary by a goon

"Great game for us. We don't go to jail. We beat up dere chicken forwards. We score 10 goals. We win. And now de Moose drinks beer."
Andre "Moose" Dupont, Philadelphia, February 9, 1973
Dupont's first language was French, but his English was much more memorable. The occasion was a 10–5 thumping of the Vancouver Canucks.

Most vivid description of being outclassed in a game

"We tried to open it up and it was like feeding a piranha."
Barry Trotz, Nashville Predators coach, December 4, 2000
A terrific turn of phrase from Trotz, who was commenting on the dangers of playing a high-tempo game against the speedy Vancouver Canucks. Like many talent-starved teams, the third-year Predators had to slow the pace to survive.

Best advice to a concussed player

"Good, tell him he's Wayne Gretzky."
Ted Green, Edmonton coach, 1990s
Green's quip after being informed that one of his players—centre Shaun Van Allen—had been knocked cold and did not know who he was.

Grossest account of a front-tooth extraction

"One was on the ice and we put that one back in. Another was up my nose and they had to pull it down."
Sami Kapanen, Philadelphia, 2003
The Finnish forward was describing how his front teeth were knocked out in a game five years earlier.

Most graphic description of a nose repair

"I grabbed it and squeezed it and put it back in place. It gave a little crunch and popped right in."
Jay Wells, NY Rangers, 1994
The Rangers defenseman was revealing how he fixed his broken beak after being high-sticked by Vancouver's Pavel Bure in Game 3 of the 1994 Cup finals.

Best description of facial scars

"He has one of those faces that holds about three days of rain."
Red Storey, NHL referee, 1950s
Storey was remembering Ted Lindsay. But opposition players were more succinct in their description of Lindsay's renowned facial wounds. They called him Scarface.

Most revealing quote about the toughness of hockey players

"Stitch me up boys, we're on a power play."
Steve Heinze, Columbus, November 2000
After being horribly slashed in the face by Brad May, Heinze hurried the Blue Jackets trainers to get him back in the game. On the ensuing man-advantage, Heinze scored a power-play goal. May received a 20-game suspension.

Most unsettling injury report

"I just came from the Canucks dressing room and Pavel's groin has never felt better."
Tom Larscheid, Vancouver radio broadcaster, 1993
The status of Pavel Bure's groin was frequently a hot topic in Vancouver.

Most mangled drug warning

"John Kordic is living proof that steroids kill."
Jean Perron, former Montreal coach-turned-broadcaster, 1992
Kordic died in 1992 after taking on six Quebec police officers in a hotel brawl. An autopsy revealed that the 27-year-old player died of heart failure induced by mixing alcohol, cocaine and steroids.

Most fatalistic remark by a repeat offender

"Just charge me with the usual."
Bob Probert, Chicago, 1994
Probert greeted police officers with this comment after crashing his motorcycle into a car. The arrest resulted in the Chicago winger being suspended for a year without pay for violating the NHL's substance abuse policy. According to police reports, Probert's blood-alcohol levels were more than three times the legal limit.

Quickest verbal comeback after being clobbered in a game

"It would have been worse if we hadn't blocked the kick after Toronto's second touchdown."
Alex Delvecchio, Detroit, 1971
Delvecchio uttered this beauty after the Maple Leafs had pulverized his Red Wings 13–0.

Least heartwarming message to the hometown fans

*"These are the people you need most. Your home base you expect
to be with you. When they turn on you, it's kind of like, well, okay,
we'll stick it up their ass too."*
Brett Hull, Detroit, 2002

Hull was irked that he and his Detroit teammates were booed off
the ice at Joe Louis Arena after dropping the first two games of
the 2002 Conference quarterfinals to the underdog Vancouver
Canucks. The Wings rallied to take the series in six games—and
stick it up everyone's ass.

Best explanation of why it's always wise to shoot

"You miss 100 per cent of the shots you don't take."
Wayne Gretzky, Edmonton, 1980s

Gretzky amassed 5,089 shots on net and 894 goals during his
fabled career.

Oddest excuse for deliberately breaking a stick

"I only have one goal in each stick."
Peter Klima, Detroit, 1980s

For a time, the eccentric Czech sniper took to superstitiously
snapping his stick after each goal he scored. Needless to say,
stick manufacturers were not lining up to get Klima to promote
their products.

Best excuse for rarely scoring

"I like to space them out so I can remember them."
Chris McAllister, Philadelphia, December 2000

The stone-handed Flyers defenseman was prepared for reporters
after he potted his first goal in 94 games.

Harshest dismissal of empty-net goals

"Empty-net goals are for faggots."
Al Iafrate, Boston, 1994

Iafrate's nickname was Crazy Horse, for obvious reasons. In this case, he was explaining to reporters why he opted to rifle the puck into the end boards rather than score into an open net during the closing seconds of a game.

Most self-deprecating remark after passing a legend on the career goal-scoring list

"It's kind of a crime because he was such an elegant player. The way he scored goals was beautiful. The way I score goals is ugly."
Pat Verbeek, Detroit, January 4, 2001

The hard-working, crease-crashing Verbeek had just scored his 508th career goal to move past Jean Béliveau into 25th place on the NHL all-time goal-scoring list.

Most grudging compliment after having a record broken

"I'm glad it's him and not some other puke."
Tiger Williams, former NHL enforcer, 2002

The always ornery Williams was asked for his thoughts after Tie Domi broke his career record for penalty minutes by a Toronto Maple Leaf.

Most insensitive remark about a cancer victim

"The Neilson situation was when Roger got cancer. That wasn't our fault. We didn't tell him to go get cancer. It's too bad that he did and we feel sorry for him, but then he went goofy on us."
Bobby Clarke, Philadelphia GM, 2000

Clarke was defending his decision to fire Neilson after his coach began cancer treatment. As he often does, Clarke created a royal stink.

Most revealing contract negotiation remark

"Listen guys, I only want to be paid what I'm worth. I'm not asking for millions. Uh, excuse me, I meant to say that . . . "
Patrice Brisebois, Montreal, September 1997
Brisebois told reporters more than he intended. The contract that the defenseman signed with Montreal was worth US$1.8 million a year.

Most amusing explanation for being released
"I didn't make enough money to stay there."
Pascal Rheaume, NY Rangers, February 2004
With a salary of only US$550,000, Rheaume was one of the lowest-paid Rangers when he was placed on waivers.

Best description of trade deadline mania

"Right now, there are so few teams selling and so many buying. It's like the Discovery Channel. Seventy-five vultures in a tree waiting for one zebra to die."
Brian Burke, Vancouver GM, March 18, 2002
The pressure to do something dramatic can melt the minds of hockey bosses at the trade deadline.

Most revealing comment by an owner

"That third quarter was really intense."
Ted Leonsis, Washington Capitals owner, October 9, 1999
After watching his team rally in the third period for a 2–2 tie with the Los Angeles Kings, Leonsis was flush with excitement. He also illustrated that it is not necessary to know much about a business before you invest hundreds of millions of dollars in it.

Most caustic postgame review

"That was a sickly, boring hockey game. Right across from our bench in the first row, there was a guy asleep on his wife's shoulder. The guy was asleep in a game with Mike Modano and Pavel Bure. I pointed it out to a whole bunch of guys. I said, 'There's another satisfied NHL customer.'"
Brett Hull, Dallas, January 20, 2001

Just one more reason why Hull will never be asked to do promotional ads for the NHL.

Strangest tribute to a hockey arena

"I loved playing there. Some guy once threw a trailer hitch at me. They're a different breed of fan, but that gets me going. I won't miss the cockroaches. I wonder how long it will take for them to cross the street."
Shane Churla, Dallas Stars, 1995

Churla was waxing nostalgic about playing in Chicago Stadium, the raucous former home of the Blackhawks. The Stadium was replaced by the United Center, which opened directly across West Madison Street in 1994.

Funniest explanation for dressing room decor

"That's so when I forget how to spell my name, I can still find my #$%@& clothes!"
Stu Grimson, Chicago, 1992

Grimson's response when asked why he kept a photo of himself above his locker.

Funniest line about hockey since Rodney Dangerfield's joke, "I went to a fight and a hockey game broke out."

"I want to tell you something, it's great being a father. I can hardly wait until I beat up my first hockey coach."

David Letterman, The Late Show with David Letterman, *November 2003*

Letterman discovered a wealth of new material when his wife gave birth to their first child.

Most arrogant comment by a first-overall draft pick

"Nobody remembers who was picked second."

Alexandre Daigle, Ottawa, 1993

Labelled the "Can't miss kid—who did," Daigle lived to regret this remark after being chosen first overall ahead of Chris Pronger (second), Chris Gratton (third) and Paul Kariya (fourth).

Most cutthroat expression of competitive spirit

"Let's put it this way: If one of my brothers were standing in front of the bus last night and we were about to leave and he was on the other team, I'd have run over him. I wouldn't have called out first to ask him to get out of the way, either. That's my mentality, that's the way it is. I don't really care."

Brian Sutter, Chicago coach, April 21, 2002

A playoff loss to the Blues put Sutter in a homicidal mood.

Best evidence that age is a state of mind

"I feel 18. If we'd lost, I'd feel dead."

Frank Mahovlich, Montreal, 1971

The 33-year-old Mahovlich was asked how he felt after Montreal's stunning upset of the first-place Boston Bruins in the 1971 playoffs.

Best reason for growing a playoff beard

"I didn't have any hair anywhere for about seven months, so now I've finally got some, I'm gonna keep it."
Saku Koivu, Montreal, 2002

After receiving chemotherapy treatments for cancer, the Habs captain was happy to need a shave.

Best insight into the mind of a player facing elimination in the playoffs

"Funny things happen when you've got a bunch of golf courses staring you in the face."
Jeff Brown, St. Louis, May 13, 1993

Brown uttered this line after his team eked out a 2–1 victory against Toronto in Game 6 of the 1993 Divisional finals. Apparently, the lure of the links got to the Blues, who absorbed a 6-0 whipping from the Leafs in Game 7.

Most accurate observation about the Stanley Cup

"This is the only thing that has seen more parties than us."
Steve Tyler, lead singer of Aerosmith, 1990s

Even hard rockers agree that the Cup rules.

CHAPTER 13

Team mismanagement

The record for the most dramatic and prolonged fall by an NHL franchise belongs to the Detroit Red Wings, who went from the lofty heights of the 1966 Stanley Cup finals to making just two playoff appearances in the next 17 years. The Dead Things did not emerge from purgatory until 1983–84, when a rookie named Steve Yzerman arrived in Motown.

Most cruelly timed franchise move
Quebec to Colorado, July 1, 1995

Would you like a little more salt in that wound? Quite a morbid sense of humour they had in Quebec City. The Nordiques ownership announced that it was moving its NHL franchise to Denver, Colorado—on Canada Day, July 1, 1995.

Worst collapse by a Stanley Cup finalist
Carolina Hurricanes, 2002–03

Cinderella stayed too long at the ball. After advancing all the way to the 2002 Cup finals, the upstart Hurricanes wound up in the ditch in 2002–03, becoming the first team since the 1925–26 Montreal Canadiens to plummet from Cup finalist to last-place overall in the span of one season. Of course, when Montreal did it there were only seven teams in the league. Twenty-nine teams were better than Carolina in 2002–03.

Longest wait to win a playoff game after joining the NHL
13 years: New Jersey Devils, 1974 to 1988

The Devils franchise began as the Kansas City Scouts in 1974, then became the Colorado Rockies in 1976 before moving to New Jersey in 1982. But it didn't matter what the team was called or in which city it played; it was a loser everywhere. The club only made the playoffs once in its first 13 years, and it wasn't until its 14th season that it finally recorded a playoff victory. The drought finally ended on April 7, 1988, when the Devils defeated the New York Islanders 3–2.

Longest wait to win at home against an opponent while wearing an original jersey

33 years: Vancouver vs. Montreal, 1970–71 to 2003–04

The hapless Canucks could not beat the Canadiens on home ice while wearing their original jerseys with the minimalist stick crest, a 21-game drought that extended from Vancouver's first season in 1970–71 until the club's switch to its garish double-V jersey in 1978–79. But more than two decades later, Vancouver got a second chance. On November 18, 2003, wearing spanking new retro jerseys, the Canucks edged the Habs 5–4 at GM Place on an overtime goal by Mattias Ohlund.

First team to take a leave of absence from the NHL

Ottawa Senators, 1931–32

Awash in red ink, the last-place Senators requested a leave of absence from the NHL at the start of the 1931–32 season. The appeal was granted and the Sens returned a year later under new management, though nothing much had changed. Ottawa finished in the cellar the next two seasons and, in 1934, the once-proud franchise was shifted to St. Louis.

First team to hold a bobble-head doll night for a player on a rival team

Pittsburgh Penguins, March 6, 2003

Despite the fact that Pittsburgh had traded star forward Alexei Kovalev to the New York Rangers a month before, the club decided to hand out 16,000 Kovalev bobble-head dolls at its March 6 game against Carolina. According to news reports, Penguins management did not want to disappoint its fans. How about not trading Kovalev in the first place? The game was a sellout, but the Pens lost 4–0.

Most costly mishandling of a goaltender

Mario Tremblay, Montreal, December 2, 1995

Tremblay, an old-school guy with absolutely no experience behind the bench, was not the right person to handle Patrick Roy. On December 2, 1995, the Montreal goalie believed he was special, and needed stroking; Tremblay felt he needed to shave off a little of Roy's ego. The Canadiens rookie coach left Roy in the net to be jeered by Montreal fans as the Red Wings pumped in nine goals. When Roy finally got the hook, he stopped by at the bench to tell Canadiens president Ronald Corey that he was through in Montreal. Roy was traded a week later to Colorado. He went on to win the Cup with the Avalanche that season, while Montreal began to disintegrate.

Only team to fire its GM and coach because of an opposition player's comments
New Jersey Devils, November 22, 1983

Even as a player, Wayne Gretzky had a lot of clout. After the Edmonton Oilers had pitchforked the Devils 13–4 on November 19, 1983, Gretzky, who had scored eight points in the game, was asked by reporters to comment on the Devils' ineptitude. The Great One didn't hold back. "It's got to a point where it isn't even funny. How long has it been for them? Three years? Five? Seven? Probably closer to nine. Well, it's time they got their act together. They're ruining the whole league. They had better stop running a Mickey Mouse organization and put somebody on ice." Three days later, New Jersey did just that, sacking its coach and GM Bill MacMillan and its director of player personnel Bert Marshall.

First owner to promise season-ticket holders a refund if the team didn't make the playoffs

Craig Leipold, Nashville Predators, 2002–03

After a poor finish in 2001–02, Predators owner Craig Leipold promised fans that 2002–03's season-ticket price increase would be refunded if the team didn't make the postseason. With the offer, Nashville attracted 83 per cent of its fans back, but the team didn't respond with the same enthusiasm. The Predators finished 24th overall and missed the playoffs, forcing Leipold to refund the ticket-price increase.

First owner to compare one of his players to Michael Jordan

Art Williams, Tampa Bay Lightning, June 1998

Williams, who made his fortune in the insurance biz, knew next to nothing about hockey, which he vividly demonstrated at the 1998 Entry Draft when he called Lightning draft pick Vincent Lecavalier "the Michael Jordan of hockey." It was quite a claim for an 18-year-old who had yet to play a single NHL game. Williams, who stated when he bought the team that he was in it "for the long haul," lasted nine months before he sold the team.

First owner to doctor his team photo

Harold Ballard, Toronto Maple Leafs, 1977

The sins of former Maple Leafs owner Harold Ballard are many. This one may rank low on the outrage scale, but it is weird nonetheless. In 1977, Ballard ordered Maple Leaf Gardens publicist Stan Obodiac to remove the beard of goalie Gord McRae from the 1977–78 team photo that appeared on the Leafs' Christmas cards. Ballard, it seems, hated beards. Obodiac had a photographer erase McRae's entire head and replace it with a clean-shaven shot of the goalie taken the year before. Needless to say, 1977–78 was McRae's last season with the Leafs.

First owner to accuse his team's doctor of conspiracy

Bill Wirtz, Chicago Blackhawks, 1997

As the Colorado Avalanche and Chicago Blackhawks duelled on the ice during the 1997 playoffs, a bizarre medical controversy was taking place behind the scenes. Chicago's team doctor, Larry Kolb, resigned during Game 3 after he was berated by Chicago owner Bill Wirtz, who was furious that Kolb had allowed Colorado's team physician, Dr. Andrew Parker, to perform arthroscopic surgery on the ankle of Chicago centre Alexei Zhamnov—without consulting management. Kolb said he asked Parker to handle the surgery because he did not have the proper licence to do the job in Colorado. When Zhamnov's ankle became infected, Wirtz accused Kolb of conspiring to undermine the team.

First merger of two NHL teams

Minnesota North Stars and Cleveland Barons, June 14, 1978

It wasn't exactly Hercules joining forces with Sampson. The bottom-feeding North Stars and Barons came together out of fiscal desperation. According to the terms of the deal, the club would be owned by Barons owners George and Gordon Gund, but would be called the North Stars and play at Minneapolis' Met Center. The influx of eight former Cleveland players did little to help Minnesota in the short term, however, as the club finished last in its division once again. But by 1981, the fast-rising North Stars had reached the Cup finals.

Most costly trade of a first-round draft pick

California Seals, 1971

One of the main purposes of the NHL Entry Draft is to allow the league's worst teams an opportunity to improve by having first crack at the best junior players. But the bumbling front office of the Seals never fully grasped the concept. The club swapped its first-round picks to Montreal in both 1970 and 1971 in exchange for aging dreck. In return for trading their first pick in the 1971 draft to Montreal, the cellar-dwelling Seals received Ernie Hicke and Montreal's first-round pick in 1970. Montreal used California's first pick to draft Guy Lafleur, the cornerstone of a future dynasty. The Seals wound up with Chris Oddleifson.

Last team accused of throwing games to get the first-overall draft pick
Ottawa Senators, 1992–93
Ottawa didn't think that finishing last overall was going to be so difficult, but found its match in the San Jose Sharks. In fact, many believe that the Senators tanked a few games to keep pace with the Sharks, who managed to lose 71 games. The prize for last place was the first draft pick. As far as the Senators were concerned, and they made it no secret, this meant Alexandre Daigle—considered the best French-Canadian junior since Mario Lemieux. As it worked out, San Jose and Ottawa settled at the bottom with 24 points, but because Ottawa had 10 wins to San Jose's 11, it got the first pick. The Sens should have tried harder: Daigle was a bust. Ottawa could have taken Chris Pronger, Paul Kariya or Todd Bertuzzi.

Most first-round draft picks traded by a team
23: Los Angeles Kings, 1967 to 2003
First-round picks have been *persona non grata* in Los Angeles since the Kings joined the NHL in 1967. They are about as common to the team as Stanley Cups, and, until Dave Taylor took over as GM in 1997, it's been a trade-our-future-for-help-

right-now philosophy. Witness the carnage: Los Angeles dealt its first original choice in 1969, 1970, 1971, 1972, 1973, 1974, 1975, 1976, 1977, 1978, 1979, 1981, 1982, 1983, 1984, 1987, 1989, 1991, 1992, 1993, 1996, 1998 and 1999—a staggering 23 times. They did acquire Wayne Gretzky for three top picks, but got fleeced on almost every other deal involving first-rounders. Players such as Ray Bourque, Steve Shutt, Ron Duguay, Mario Tremblay, Reggie Leach, Scott Stevens, Phil Housley and Tom Barrasso were all first-round picks that other teams drafted in the position the Kings dealt away. L.A. could have had quite a team; but instead it landed stiffs such as Skip Krake, Gerry Desjardins, Gene Carr and Glenn Goldup. In a few cases, Los Angeles improved its first-round position in trades with other teams, but still got stung, as in 1984, when Chicago got Ed Olczyk (originally an L.A. pick) and the Kings took Craig Redmond. Truly pathetic.

Most costly late-season winning streak
Vancouver Canucks, 1970–71

There is honour and then there is stupidity. The Canucks cobbled together a brief late-season winning streak in 1970–71 that enabled them to slip past Detroit by a single point in the standings. By finishing ahead of the Red Wings, Vancouver picked third in the draft rather than second. The difference was monumental. Detroit selected Marcel Dionne; the Canucks got Jocelyn Guevremont.

Only team to have a rival team play the home opener at its new rink
Montreal Maroons, November 29, 1924

The Montreal Forum was built to house the Montreal Maroons, who joined the NHL in 1924–25. However, because the natural ice at the Montreal Canadiens' home rink, the Mount Royal Arena, was not ready in time for their season opener, the Maroons' crosstown rival played the first game at the Forum (a 7–1 win over the Toronto St. Pats), in November 1924. The Canadiens did not move into the Forum on a full-time basis until 1926–27.

Most home games played by a team in another country
22: Detroit Cougars, 1926–27
Because their home rink, Olympia Stadium, was still under construction, the Detroit Cougars played all their home games in their first NHL season at the Border City Arena in Windsor, Ontario. The Olympia finally opened for business on November 22, 1927.

First American-based NHL franchise to move to Canada
Atlanta Flames to Calgary, 1980
Although they played in a place where hockey was a novelty, the Flames iced some decent teams during their eight years in Dixie. But any chance the club had of becoming a hit at the box office was torpedoed by its inability to win a single playoff series. In 1980, Atlanta's majority owner, Tom Cousins, sold the franchise to Vancouver businessman Nelson Skalbania for US$16 million, a record price for an NHL team at the time.

Only team to change its name to try and capitalize on the popularity of a baseball team
Brooklyn Americans, 1941–42
With home attendance waning and a roster decimated by World War II call-ups, New York Americans GM Red Dutton changed his team's name to the Brooklyn Americans in a bid to capitalize on the popularity of the Brooklyn Dodgers baseball team, even though his club played in Manhattan. It didn't help. Brooklyn

finished last in 1941–42, just as it had the previous season, and the franchise folded.

Most owners of one team
37: Edmonton Oilers, 1999–2000
In 1988, the "City of Champions" saw its cash-strapped hockey team put up for sale, and a group of 17 local investors raised enough money to buy the franchise and keep it in Edmonton. But by the time the 1999–2000 season began, the rapidly expanding ownership group had 37 members. This complicated situation did not sit well with GM Glen Sather, who stated: "I hate to say this, but it won't work." The front-office log-jam led to Sather leaving the club at the end of the season.

Most heart transplants needed by a team
18: Chicago Blackhawks, 1983
Fiery rookie coach Orval Tessier lit a blaze under the 1982–83 Blackhawks, leading the club to 47 wins and first place in the Norris Division, but the heat didn't last. After the Hawks had disposed of the St. Louis Blues and Minnesota North Stars in the first two playoff rounds, they ran into a tougher obstacle: Wayne Gretkzy and the Edmonton Oilers. The Oilers pounded Chicago 8–4 and 8–2 in the first two games of the Western Conference finals, prompting a frustrated Tessier to publicly rip his players, saying they "needed 18 heart transplants." The slight didn't go over well with his team, which was swept in four straight. Tessier and the Hawks never recovered. The next season, many of Chicago's players stopped playing for Tessier, who was sent packing in 1984–85.

Most players lost by a team to military service

28: New York Rangers, 1941–42 to 1943–44

All NHL teams lost players to the war effort in the early 1940s, but the hardest hit was the Rangers, who watched 28 players leave to join the armed services in a span of three seasons. The mass exodus reached crisis proportions in 1943–44, when New York, with only six returning players from the previous year, activated coach Frank Boucher, who had been retired for five years. The Rangers got off to a 0–14–1 start, the worst by any team in NHL history, and finished with a miserable 6–39–5 record.

Most coaches fired by a team in its first 10 years of existence

13: Chicago Blackhawks, 1926–27 to 1936–37

Blackhawks owner Frederic McLaughlin was called many things in his lifetime, but patient wasn't one of them. During Chicago's first decade, the millionaire coffee baron hired and fired 13 coaches. In 1932–33, he used three bench bosses in one season—and the schedule was only 48 games! McLaughlin even gassed Tommy Gorman immediately after he coached Chicago to its first Cup in 1934. Unable to stand prosperity, McLaughlin also sent Bill Stewart packing only 21 games after he led the Hawks to their second Cup in 1938.

Most games played by a team without a GM, one season

65: Vancouver Canucks, 1997–98

In the weird West Coast twilight that followed the firing of Pat Quinn as GM and the hiring of Mike Keenan as coach in November 1997, the Canucks played the rest of the season without a general manager. Instead, a management committee was formed consisting of team president Stephen Bellringer; vice-president of hockey operations Steve Tambellini; head scout

Mike Penny, and Keenan. With no boss to reign him in, Keenan soon seized the lion's share of power and embarked on a manic purge. Long-time fan favourites such as Trevor Linden, Kirk McLean and Gino Odjick were hastily traded, and the team sank to the depths of the league. It was not until June 1998, when Brian Burke was hired as GM, that the chaos was finally cleared.

Most expensive team failure
New York Rangers, 2003–04
In 2003–04, influential *New York Times* columnist Dave Anderson pronounced the Rangers "dollar for dollar, the worst team in any sport in any era." That's not the sort of description that GM Glen Sather had in mind when he assumed command of the Broadway Blueshirts in June 2000. For all his supposed genius, Sather did nothing to turn around this titanic disaster. Spending even more wildly than his predecessors, he stacked up on US$90 million worth of superstars and they, in turn, stacked up the losses. Not only was Sather a front-office failure, he bombed as a coach too. Shortly after moving behind the bench in 2002–03, he vowed the club would make the playoffs— it didn't. Finally, late in 2003–04, he stepped down from the coaching post, chased away by the incessant chant of "Fire Sather!" that greeted him at every Rangers home game.

CHAPTER 14

Trail
to the grail

Ray Bourque and Chris Hayes both skated for Boston, but Hayes played only one NHL game—a semifinals match in 1972 that got his name stamped on the Stanley Cup. Bourque? He toiled a record 214 playoff games before lifting Stanley in 2001 with Colorado during a chase he called Mission 16w—16 playoff wins to the Cup. The trail to the Grail is different for everyone, but, for some, luck leads the way.

Most playoff goal-scoring titles

5: Maurice Richard, 1943 to 1960

Richard existed to score goals, and in the playoffs, his maniacal drive intensified. As Frank Selke, former managing director of the Canadiens once said about Richard: "When he's worked up his eyes gleam like headlights—not a glow, but a burning intensity. Goalies have said he's like a motor car coming at you at night. It's terrifying." The Rocket's 82 playoff goals held up until 1985, when Mike Bossy equalled and later passed his mark as career leader. Still, Bossy never managed more than three goal-scoring titles to Richard's five. Richard led the postseason in 1944, 1946, 1947, 1951 and 1958, his last title coming 14 years after his first, the longest span of any goal leader in playoff action.

Most consecutive playoff games scoring a goal

8: Maurice Richard, Montreal, March 27, 1945 to March 30, 1946

There was little that stopped the Punch Line in its heyday. Toe Blake, Elmer Lach and Maurice Richard could usually be counted on to deliver the knockout blow. Richard, the line's trigger man, tallied 11 goals in eight straight playoff matches, a record that has not been matched, and his goal in the eighth game proved to be the first of his three NHL-record career-overtime winners. It clinched a 4–3 win over Boston in Game 1 of the 1946 finals, a series that Montreal went on to win to claim its second Cup in three years.

Most consecutive game-winning goals, one series

3: several players

Mike Bossy nailed four game winners in one series and fellow New York Islander Clark Gillies had four straight in one playoff year, but the record for consecutive winners in a series belongs to Martin St. Louis (2003), Kevin Stevens (1991), Gillies (1977) and Roy Conacher (1939). Each scored three, with St. Louis notching his third in triple-overtime against Washington, to give Tampa Bay its first playoff series win in franchise history.

Most series-deciding overtime goals, career
3: Martin Gelinas, 1990 to 2004

They dubbed Gelinas the Eliminator after he became the first NHLer to end three playoff series with overtime goals. Carolina reached the 2002 Stanley Cup final by knocking off Toronto thanks to his Conference final winner in overtime. Then, in 2004, the Calgary Flames eliminated Vancouver in the first round and Detroit in the second with back-to-back series overtime winners, again by Gelinas. His record-setting third series-ending overtime goal was scored on a rebound against goalie Curtis Joseph at 19:13 of the extra period. "It was a great team game," said Gelinas. "I'm happy to be in the right place. If it wasn't me, it would have been one of my teammates." Spoken like a true playoff warrior.

First player to score a playoff penalty-shot goal
Wayne Connelly, Minnesota, April 9, 1968

Fifty years after the NHL staged its first playoff game, Connelly scored the league's first goal on a penalty shot. It was awarded after Dale Rolfe interfered with the North Star forward on a clean break against Los Angeles Kings goalie Terry Sawchuk. Connelly made no mistake, skating straight in and roofing it over Sawchuk. Three previous attempts—by Lionel Conacher and Alex Shibicky in 1937 and Virgil Johnson in 1944—all failed.

First player to score an overtime playoff goal
Odie Cleghorn, Montreal, March 30, 1919

Cleghorn potted the sudden-death winner against goalie Hap Holmes of the Seattle Metropolitans in a 4–3 Canadiens win in Game 5 of the 1919 Cup finals. It was the last game played that year. A flu epidemic cancelled the round, leaving the NHL without a Cup winner for the only time in its history.

Age of youngest player to score an overtime playoff goal
17.11 years: Don Gallinger, Boston, March 21, 1943

The Bruins were on a youth kick in 1942–43. Gallinger began the season centreing the Sprout Line with 16-year-old Bep Guidolin and 19-year-old Bill Shill. Gallinger's overtime winner beat Montreal 5–4 in the first game of the 1943 semifinals.

Age of oldest player to score an overtime playoff goal
41.6: Igor Larionov, Detroit, June 8, 2002

Larionov ended a triple-overtime game with a goal against Carolina in the 2003 Cup finals. The 41-year-old Russian must have been using super vitamins.

Longest drought between playoff goals
11 years: Craig Ludwig, 1988 to 1999
10 years: Harry Howell, 1959 to 1968
10 years: Johnny Bucyk, 1959 to 1969
10 years: Gordie Howe, 1970 to 1980

Unlike the others on this list, Ludwig had plenty of chances: his teams reached the postseason six times during his 11-year scoring hiatus. The stay-at-home defenseman counted just four goals in 177 career playoff games. At age 38, Ludwig broke his drought on June 10, 1999, in a 4–2 Dallas win over Buffalo. Asked after the game, "When was the last time you scored a playoff goal?" Ludwig deadpanned: "It was just a few minutes ago. Didn't you see it?"

Most playoff hat tricks, career
10: Wayne Gretzky, 1980 to 1999
7: Maurice Richard, 1944 to 1960
7: Jari Kurri, 1981 to 1998
The biggest difference between these three? Gretzky played 208 postseason games; Kurri, 200; Richard, 133. Gretzky upped his total to a perfect 10 with two tricks for the Rangers in the 1997 playoffs.

First defenseman to lead all scorers, one playoff year
Al MacInnis, Calgary, 1989
Only two defensemen have amassed more points than all scorers in one playoff year: Brian Leetch in 1994, and MacInnis, whose MVP performance in 1989 led Calgary to its lone Stanley Cup. MacInnis collected 31 points on seven goals and 24 assists. And 26 of those points came during MacInnis's 17-game consecutive point-scoring streak—one game shy of the record for one playoff year, set by Bryan Trottier.

Only player to lead the playoffs in scoring and penalty minutes
Maurice Richard, Montreal, 1947
The smart money says this record won't be matched. In 1947, Richard paced all playoff shooters with 11 points on six goals and five assists and also led with 44 penalty minutes—more than half of them picked up in Game 2 of the finals against Toronto, when he slashed shut the eye of Vic Lynn and sliced open Bill Ezinicki's skull. The second foul earned Richard a 20-minute

match misconduct. Richard repeated as the playoff leader in penalty minutes in 1956. By doing so, he preserved his record. Richard's 24 PIM was two more minutes than that year's playoffs scoring leader, teammate Jean Béliveau accumulated.

Most regular-season games for a championship team by a player who did not get his name on the Cup

72: Don Awrey, Montreal, 1975–76
71: Mike Gartner, NY Rangers, 1993–94

Awrey played 72 of 80 games for the Cup-winning Canadiens in 1975–76, but did not see any ice time in the playoffs. At the time, NHL rules stipulated that a player had to play in the finals in order to have his name enscribed on the Cup. The rule was changed after this incident, but that didn't help Awrey. Although he dressed for all four games of the finals against Philadelphia, coach Scotty Bowman declined to give Awrey even one shift. Fortunately, the defenseman did get his name on the Cup in 1970 and 1972 with the Boston Bruins. Gartner played 71 games for the Cup-winning Rangers before the club traded him to Toronto late in the 1993–94 campaign.

First player to win the Stanley Cup while attending high school

Gaye Stewart, Toronto, 1942

Imagine Stewart's status with the rest of his classmates. The 18-year-old began the 1941–42 season playing junior hockey with the Toronto Marlboros, then was promoted to the Hershey Bears of the American Hockey League before finally getting the call by the Maple Leafs during the playoffs. He suited up for one game in the finals as Toronto staged the biggest comeback in playoff history, rallying from three games down to defeat Detroit. After sipping champagne from the Cup, Stewart returned to high school.

Only NHL player to win the Stanley Cup and the Grey Cup

Lionel Conacher, 1926 to 1937

Conacher was a standout in hockey, baseball, football, boxing, lacrosse and track and field, though by most accounts, hockey was his worst sport. The Big Train won the 1921 Grey Cup with the Toronto Argonauts and claimed the Stanley Cup in 1934 with Chicago and in 1935 with the Montreal Maroons.

Only NHL player to appear in a Stanley Cup and Grey Cup final in the same year

Gerry James, 1960

Known as "Kid Dynamite," James signed with the CFL's Winnipeg Blue Bombers at age 17, becoming the league's youngest player. While playing pro football, James also played junior hockey with the Toronto Marlboros, winning the Memorial Cup in 1955 before joining the Toronto Maple Leafs. The running back would make six trips to the Grey Cup, winning four times. In 1960, he won the Grey Cup with the Blue Bombers, then joined the Maple Leafs, who reached the Stanley Cup finals before losing to Montreal.

Only player to win the Cup with two New York teams

Greg Gilbert, NY Islanders, 1982 and 1983; NY Rangers, 1994

Although the Rangers and the Americans played in the NHL together for 15 seasons, the Americans never won a Cup, narrowing the window of opportunity for a player to win a Cup with two New York-based teams to the Rangers and Islanders. Gilbert is the only man to do it. He bagged two Cups with the Isles in the 1980s, then, later in his career, joined the Rangers for one season and won his third in 1994.

Only player to win the Cup with two Montreal NHL teams

Toe Blake, Montreal Maroons, 1935; Montreal Canadiens, 1944 and 1946

Before the Canadiens developed great rivalries with Toronto, Detroit, Quebec and Boston, they faced the Maroons, a crosstown matchup designed to pit English against French in bilingual Montreal. It was a bitter rivalry, and, as a result, the Maroons and Canadiens seldom traded players. One exception was Blake, who won his first Cup as a rookie with the Maroons in 1935. He was traded the next season and began his historic tenure as a player and, later, as coach of the Canadiens, winning championships in 1944 and 1946 before capturing another eight Cups as bench boss.

Most consecutive games by a goalie against the same team from start of playoff career

21: Tommy Salo, 1999 to 2003

Somehow you get the feeling that Salo doesn't have warm feelings about Texas. His first four playoff series were all against Dallas, and his team, the Oilers, was defeated each time (1999, 2000, 2001 and 2003). Salo's record in the 21 games was five wins and 16 losses, which was about the same as his career regular-season mark versus Dallas: 4–14–1. The Oilers dealt Salo to Colorado at the 2003–04 trade deadline. He saw only 26 minutes of postseason action with Colorado, but for the first time he suited up against a club other than Dallas: 26 minutes against the San Jose Sharks. Colorado was eliminated in six games, keeping another of Salo's streaks intact—never playing for a team that has won a playoff series.

Most consecutive wins by a goalie from start of playoff career

7: Tiny Thompson, Boston, 1929 and 1930

6: Jean-Sebastien Giguere, Anaheim, 2003

Penguins goalie Tom Barrasso owns the NHL mark for consecutive playoff victories, with 14 in 1992 and 1993, but Thompson had the most successful start to a playoff career. The Boston goalkeeper earned five straight wins and the Stanley Cup in 1929—and another two wins to start the 1930 playoffs—before he was finally beaten 1–0 by the Montreal Maroons in double overtime on March 25, 1930. Giguere came within a game of tying Thompson, winning his first six playoff contests in 2003.

Most consecutive losses by a goalie from start of playoff career

10: Dan Bouchard, Atlanta, 1974 to 1980

Ouch! The Flames kept sending Bouchard out there, and he kept coming back with his tail between his legs. But after 10 straight losses, he finally got to celebrate with a 4–2 victory over the Rangers in Game 3 of the 1980 preliminary round. It was Bouchard's only playoff win for Atlanta. The Flames lost the next game and the series, and the franchise moved to Calgary the next season.

Longest overtime shutout sequence, one playoff year

168:27: J.S. Giguere, Anaheim, 2003

Although George Hainsworth holds the record for the longest shutout sequence in one playoff year, Giguere made his mark with seven straight overtime wins in the 2003 playoffs. The Mighty Duck goaltender posted victories against Detroit at 43:18 and 6:53 of overtime; against Dallas at 80:48 and 1:44; against Minnesota at 28:06; and against New Jersey at 6:59 and 0:39.

Longest shutout sequence by a goalie, one playoff year

Length	Goalie	Team	Dates
270:08	George Hainsworth	Mtl.	March 28 to April 3, 1930
248:35	Dave Kerr	NYR	March 25 to April 6, 1937
248:32	Normie Smith	Det.	March 24 to 28, 1936
218:42	Gerry McNeil	Mtl.	March 27 to 31, 1951
217:54	J.S. Giguere	Ana.	May 5 to 16, 2003

Fewest goals allowed, one series (since 1939)

1: Jean-Sebastien Giguere, Anaheim, 2003
2: Terry Sawchuk, Detroit, 1952

After downing Detroit and Dallas in the first two rounds of 2003, Anaheim stopped the Minnesota Wild with three straight zeros in the Conference finals. In Game 4, Giguere allowed just one goal as Andrew Brunette connected at 4:47 of the first period. The goal ended Giguere's shutout run at 217:44, the fifth longest in history.

Most combined goals allowed by opposing goalies, one game

18: Grant Fuhr, Edmonton; Mario Lessard, Los Angeles,
April 7, 1982

Edmonton and Los Angeles have a history of goal orgies in the playoffs, but particularly in 1982 and 1987, when they amassed a league-leading 50 and 52 goals respectively in a five-game series. In their first playoff matchup ever, the clubs established an all-time NHL high of 18 goals in a 10–8 Kings win.

Most saves by a goalie, one game

113: Tiny Thompson, Boston, April 3–4, 1933

In our first *Unofficial Guide,* we reported that the longest NHL game, a March 1936 playoff tilt between the Maroons and the Red Wings, produced the most shots against a goalie. But further research has revealed that Detroit's Normie Smith, who stopped 90 shots in that 1–0 win, is not the record holder. More rubber was fired at Boston's Tiny Thompson and Toronto's Lorne Chabot in the NHL's second-longest game in April 1933. Thompson broke the triple-digit barrier with 113 saves while Chabot turned back 93 in the 1–0 Toronto win. The exhausted goalies combined to stop a record 206 shots during six overtime periods, playing 164 minutes and 46 seconds of shutout hockey. Because the winning team had to play in the finals in New York that same night, NHL president Frank Calder suggested after the fifth overtime period that a coin toss decide the winner. Boston agreed but Toronto elected to play on. The Maple Leafs prevailed in the sixth overtime when 124-pound winger Ken Doraty, the smallest player on the ice, scored at 1:48 AM.

Most generous gesture by a losing goalie, one game

Lorne Chabot, Montreal Maroons, March 25, 1936

Several hours after the Maroons and the Red Wings finished playing hockey's longest game, a six-overtime playoff marathon that finally ended when Maroons goalie Lorne Chabot was beaten by rookie winger Mud Bruneteau in a 1–0 loss, Chabot showed up in the lobby of the hotel where the Red Wings were staying and presented a gift to Detroit coach Jack Adams. "Give it to the kid," said Chabot. "It's the puck he shot past me for that winning goal. I thought he'd like to have it."

Most playoff games coached, career

353: Scotty Bowman, 1967 to 2002
209: Al Arbour, 1970 to 1994

Bowman stuck around long enough to beat Toe Blake's record of eight Cups and set this record of 353 games. Amazingly, Bowman's record of 223 wins is more than the 209 total games coached by his nearest competitor, Arbour.

Most playoff ties by a coach, career

7: Lester Patrick, 1926 to 1939
5: Art Ross, 1917 to 1945

Here's a record that Patrick will hold forever. He set the mark for ties with the New York Rangers during an era in which many playoff series were decided by total goals and games could end without a winner being declared.

Most combined career wins by opposing coaches, one series

1,579: Scotty Bowman and Al Arbour, 1993

Bowman's Pittsburgh Penguins and Arbour's New York Islanders clashed in the 1993 Patrick Division finals. At the time, Bowman had an NHL-leading 834 career wins and Arbour had 745. Arbour's underdog Isles prevailed in dramatic fashion, taking the series on a Game 7 overtime goal by David Volek.

Most playoff games coached before winning a Cup

120: Pat Burns, 1989 to 2004
117: Mike Keenan, 1985 to 2004

Until Burns won it all with New Jersey in 2003, he was headed for Pat Quinn country: most playoff games coached without a Cup. Now he leads Keenan in this category: longest wait before winning it all.

Most one-goal wins by a team, one playoff year

12: Montreal Canadiens, 1993
12: Anaheim Mighty Ducks, 2003

Anaheim's Jean-Sebastien Giguere and his mentor Patrick Roy
both turned in Conn Smythe-winning performances, but Roy
and the Canadiens didn't have to face the 2003 New Jersey Devils
in the finals. Montreal beat Los Angeles in five and took home
the Cup in 1993; while Giguere pushed New Jersey to seven
before losing 3–0.

Only team to defeat the defending Cup champions in three consecutive playoff years

Detroit Red Wings, 1941, 1942, 1943

The Wings played the role of giant killers in three straight postseasons. In 1941, Detroit upset the defending champion Rangers
in the quarterfinals before being beaten by Boston in the finals.
In 1942, Detroit torpedoed the Cup champion Bruins in the
semifinals, only to lose to Toronto in the finals. In 1943, Detroit
defeated the champion Maple Leafs in the semifinals, then went
on to sweep Boston in the finals to claim the Cup.

Fastest demise of a franchise after winning the Cup
3 years: Montreal Maroons, 1938

From the penthouse to the trash bin in three short seasons. Beset
by economic woes, the Maroons traded several stars after their
1935 Cup victory but still remained competitive, qualifying for the
playoffs for the next two years. But after a last-place finish in 1938,
the cash-strapped club suddenly folded, leaving the Montreal Forum
to the Canadiens.

Most regular-season points out of first place by a Cup-winning team

32: Montreal Canadiens, 1986

One of Montreal's most unexpected Cup winners, the Canadiens managed to claim the crown despite a very ordinary 87-point regular season—32 points behind first-place Edmonton. Fate favoured the Habs during the playoffs, as each of the league's top clubs were eliminated while seventh-place Montreal met weaker teams in every round except the finals, when it faced the sixth-place Calgary Flames. Of course, a rookie named Patrick Roy didn't hurt.

Only team to win the Cup with the worst power play in the league
New Jersey Devils, 2003

Everyone knows you can't win the Cup without an effective power play. But everyone is wrong. The Devils took home the silver bowl despite an anemic power play that capitalized on just 36 goals in 303 chances during the 2002–03 regular season, a feeble 11.9 per cent efficiency rate. By comparison, Detroit, which was swept in the first round, led the league, capitalizing on 23.8 per cent of its man-advantages.

Only team to play two playoff games against two different teams on the same day
Toronto Maple Leafs, April 4, 1933

Toronto and Boston battled to the point of exhaustion in the longest game ever played at Maple Leaf Gardens, an epic struggle in Game 5 of the 1933 semifinals that lasted 164 minutes, 46 seconds. The tilt ended 1–0 in the sixth period of overtime at 1:48 AM, but the Leafs had no time to celebrate. They had to rush to board a train to New York to play the first game of the finals, scheduled for that evening. Toronto arrived in Manhattan late in the afternoon, bleary with fatigue, and dropped the series opener to the Rangers 5–1. After a three-day break, the teams returned to Toronto for the rest of the best-of-five series, which New York took three games to one.

Most home-ice wins, one playoff year

12: New Jersey Devils, 2003

Since the advent of the four rounds, best-of-seven-series format in 1987, no Cup champion had swept all its home games—until 2003. The Devils were an overpowering 12–1 at Continental Airlines Arena.

Most road wins, one playoff year

10: New Jersey Devils, 1995
10: New Jersey Devils, 2000
10: Calgary Flames, 2004

Had the Flames, who went 10–4 on the road, been able to beat Tampa Bay in Game 7 of the 2004 finals, they would own this record outright. But they lost 2–1 and the Cup went south. The Devils were 10–1 in 1995 and 10–2 in 2000 on the road, winning the Cup both years.

Most consecutive playoff eliminations

10: Montreal Canadiens, 1932 to 1943
9: Winnipeg Jets/Phoenix Coyotes, 1987 to 2003

In Montreal, they call this period *"la Grande Noirceur,"* or the Great Darkness. The cloud finally lifted with the formation of the Punch Line, with Elmer Lach, Toe Blake and Maurice Richard. In 1943–44, the high-scoring trio led Montreal to the

Cup. The Coyotes haven't coined a name for their bleak postseason stretch, but it stings all the same.

Most consecutive playoff losses

16: Chicago Blackhawks, 1975 to 1979
14: Los Angeles Kings, 1993 to 2003
12: Toronto Maple Leafs, 1979 to 1983

Chicago's record-setting run of ineptitude began on April 20, 1975, with a loss to Buffalo in the quarterfinals, and didn't end until April 8, 1980, when the Hawks defeated St. Louis in overtime in the first game of the preliminary round.

Longest playoff series in total playing time

Nine hours, 13 minutes, eight seconds: NY Rangers vs. Boston, 1939
Eight hours, 52 minutes, five seconds: Toronto vs. Philadelphia, 2003

The Rangers and Bruins battled through eight overtime periods in their gruelling seven-game death match in the 1939 semifinals. The series included four overtime games and a pair of triple-overtime marathons, the first in Game 1 and the second in Game 7, which Boston won 2–1 on a goal by rookie winger Mel Hill at 48:00 of overtime.

CHAPTER 15

Kissing
your sister

Dino Ciccarelli doesn't immediately

spring to mind when one thinks

of big playoff scorers. But he should. His 73 goals

rank ahead of the totals posted by scoring legends

Gordie Howe, Bobby Hull and Yvan Cournoyer.

Still, high-ranking numbers didn't win Ciccarelli

the Stanley Cup, which is like kissing your sister

instead of planting one on Lord Stanley's mug.

Most goals by a defenseman who did not win a Cup, career
35: Brad Park, 1969 to 1985

Paul Coffey, Denis Potvin, Ray Bourque and Al MacInnis: all of Park's fellow high-scoring rearguards own a Cup. Park is without peer in playoff futility, a Cup-less phenomenon of great talent who deserved better than this fate. Not only does he own the record for most goals (35) by a Cup-less defenseman, but he can also claim most assists (90), most points (125), most games (161) and most consecutive playoff years (17).

Most goals by a player who did not win a Cup, one playoff year
19: Reggie Leach, Philadelphia, 1976

Philadelphia's whipping at the hands of Montreal in the 1976 Cup finals came with a few perks for Reggie the Rifle. Never one to accept personal gain over team success, Leach's consolation prize was two league records: most playoff goals and longest consecutive goal-scoring streak in one playoff year; plus the Conn Smythe Trophy as playoff MVP.

Most goals by a defenseman who did not win a Cup, one playoff year
9: Brad Park, Boston, 1978

Park totalled nine goals in 15 games and he might have been the most dominant rearguard on the ice, except for one thing: his Bruins didn't take home the Cup. That honour went to Montreal and Larry Robinson, who was named playoff MVP with 21 points, just one more than Park.

Most assists by a player who did not win a Cup, career

114: Adam Oates, 1968 to 2004

As many playoff assists as Oates amassed with Detroit, St. Louis, Boston and Washington and Philadelphia, he never got closer to a Stanley Cup than when he recorded his final nine helpers with Anaheim in 2003. The Mighty Ducks and Oates came within a whisker of a championship, only to go down to New Jersey in seven during the finals.

Most assists by a player who did not win a Cup, one playoff year

26: Wayne Gretzky, Edmonton, 1983

The young, upstart Edmonton Oilers learned more about commitment and what it takes to win the Cup during the 1983 finals against the New York Islanders than in any other playoff round. Gretzky led all scorers with 38 points—including 26 assists, four of which came on six Edmonton goals during the finals. After New York had swept Edmonton, Gretzky and Kevin Lowe had to walk past the Islanders' dressing room door to get to their bus. They expected to hear hollers and shouts of celebration. Instead, the veteran team was in repair mode. "Guys were limping around with black eyes and bloody mouths," remembers Gretzky in his biography *Gretzky.* "It looked more like a morgue in there than a champion's locker room. And here we were, perfectly fine and healthy. And that's when Kevin said something I will never forget. He said: 'That's how you win championships.' "

Most assists by a player on a losing team, one series

11: Al MacInnis, Calgary, 1984
11: Mark Messier, Edmonton, 1989
11: Mike Ridley, Washington, 1992

All three players were team scoring leaders in series that went seven games against hockey's most dominant stars:

Wayne Gretzky and Mario Lemieux. MacInnis and Messier couldn't hold back Edmonton and Los Angeles, two Gretzky-led teams, and Ridley's Capitals lost to Pittsburgh. Both the Oilers in 1984 and the Penguins in 1992 claimed the Cup.

Most assists by a defenseman who did not win a Cup, one playoff year
18: Raymond Bourque, Boston, 1988 and 1991

These numbers say so much about why Bourque's lone Cup with Colorado in 2001 was so important. His Hall of Fame career cried out for a championship after twice being denied in Cup finals action (1988 and 1990). His 18-point tally in 1988 and, again, in 1991, is the most by a Cup-less blueliner in one season.

Most points by a player who did not win a Cup, career
156: Adam Oates, 1986 to 2004

Like Brad Park, Oates has had a career of playoff frustration. While Park leads rearguards in many records for Cup-less players, Oates owns the assists and points records and is second to Dale Hunter in games played. Oates has 163 games to Hunter's 186.

Most points by a player who did not win a Cup, one playoff year
40: Wayne Gretzky, Los Angeles, 1993

Gretzky carried the Kings through four gruelling playoff rounds and 24 games before capitulating to Montreal in 1993. It was Gretzky's only real opportunity at another Cup after his dynasty years in Edmonton; and he took his best shot with 15 goals and 25 assists.

Most points by a defenseman who did not win a Cup, one playoff year

25: Ray Bourque, Boston, 1991

Bourque's seven goals and 18 assists represent his best playoff year—and the Bruins didn't even make it to the finals. Mario Lemieux and Pittsburgh stopped Boston cold in six games during the Conference finals.

Most goals by a player who did not win a Cup, one series

11: Newsy Lalonde, Montreal, 1919
10: Tim Kerr, Philadelphia, 1989

Lalonde scored 11 goals in Montreal's playoff series win against Ottawa, then added six more in five games in the finals against the Seattle Metropolitans before an outbreak of Spanish Influenza forced the cancellation of the deciding game. The series was abandoned with no Cup winner declared. Seventy years later, Tim Kerr paced the Flyers with 10 goals to no avail in a seven-game knock-'em-down, drag-'em-out series against Pittsburgh.

Most goals by a player on a losing team, one series

9: Mario Lemieux, Pittsburgh, 1989

If any playoff year was a harbinger of success for Pittsburgh, it was 1989. Lemieux captained the Penguins to their first playoffs in six years with a sweep of the New York Rangers. In the next series, the Flyers needed seven games to eliminate Lemieux, who scored nine goals in the losing cause. In their next trip to the playoffs, in 1991, the Penguins won it all—led by Lemieux and his 44 points.

Most goals by a player in an overtime loss

4: Lanny McDonald, Toronto, April 17, 1977

With his team ahead 2–1 in games, McDonald came out with guns blazing as he tried to bury Philadelphia and establish a commanding 3–1 series lead. Instead, his four goals were wasted: Toronto lost 6–5 in overtime. The Maple Leafs never recovered, giving up the next two games and the round to the Flyers.

Most goals by a player on a losing team, one game

4: Lanny McDonald, Toronto, April 17, 1977
4: Denis Savard, Chicago, April 10, 1986
4: Ray Ferraro, NY Islanders, April 26, 1993

It's been known to happen: score a hat trick and still lose a playoff game. But four goals! How do you make nice after that? McDonald's Maple Leafs lost 6–5 to Philadelphia; Savard's Blackhawks went down 6–4 to Toronto, and Ferraro's Islanders were beaten 6–4 by Washington.

Most goals by a player in a Cup-losing game

3: Frank Boucher, NY Rangers, April 9, 1932
3: Pit Martin, Chicago, May 10, 1973
3: Dirk Graham, Chicago, June 1, 1992

Bobby Hull once scored three goals for Chicago during a game that ended the Hawks' postseason, but that was in semifinal action. Imagine scoring a hat trick and losing the Cup? Surprisingly, it has happened to a hat trick of players: Boucher, Martin and Graham. Boucher's Rangers lost 6–4 in the deciding game of a best-of-five series against Toronto, handing the Maple Leafs their first Cup. Martin scored three times against Ken Dryden, yet the Blackhawks lost 6–4 to Montreal. Graham's hat trick also had no impact, as Chicago lost 6–5 and was swept four straight by the champion Penguins.

Most goals by a defenseman on a losing team, one game

3: Paul Reinhart, Calgary, April 14, 1983
3: Brian Leetch, NY Rangers, May 22, 1995

Among the 24 players who scored three-or-more goals in a losing cause, Leetch and Reinhart are the only defensemen. But Leetch may have endured the worst fate under such circumstances, scoring his team's only three goals then losing in overtime 4–3. His Rangers never got back in it, giving up consecutive matches and bowing to Philadelphia four straight. Reinhart scored Calgary's first three goals of its series against Edmonton, but the 6–3 loss sealed Calgary's fate as Gretzky's Oilers doused the Flames in five.

Most power-play goals by a player who did not win a Cup, one playoff year

9: Cam Neely, Boston, 1991

To date, Neely shares the NHL record with Mike Bossy for most power-play goals in a postseason. But Neely could have made this one his own had the Bruins got past Pittsburgh in the third round. Instead, his record has a black cloud hanging over it.

Most power-play goals by a player on a losing team, one series

5: four players

Rick Vaive, Mario Lemieux, Pat LaFontaine and Doug Weight all scored five power-play goals in series that saw their teams eliminated. Los Angeles' Chris Kontos leads all NHLers with six power-play goals in one series, but his team won.

Most game-winning goals by a player who did not win a Cup, one playoff year

5: Bobby Smith, Minnesota, 1991

Before succumbing to Pittsburgh in six games in the 1991 finals, Smith tallied five game winners in 14 victories by the North Stars. Not bad for a guy who was never a recognized sniper.

Most game-winning goals by a rookie who did not win a Cup, one playoff year

4: Chris Drury, Colorado, 1999

With the exception of Claude Lemieux in 1986, Drury is the only other rookie with four game winners in a playoff season. Fortunately for Lemieux, he didn't share Drury's misfortune. Colorado fell apart after taking a 3–2 series lead against the Stars in the Conference finals.

Most overtime goals by a player who did not win a Cup, career

4: Dale Hunter, 1980–81 to 1998–99

Hunter pushed, punched and hacked every player on every shift of every game for Quebec and Washington through 19 years, but only reached the finals once, in 1998, when Detroit swept his Cinderella Capitals in four games. In 1999, Colorado rented Hunter for its playoff run, but the Avalanche lost momentum before the finals. The pit bull retired later that summer.

Most overtime goals by a player who did not win a Cup, one playoff year

3: Maurice Richard, Montreal, 1951

Richard's only remaining playoff record of six overtime goals is marred by Montreal's losing effort in 1951, when the Rocket recorded half of his career total. He scored two overtime winners against Detroit in the semifinals and another in the finals as the Canadiens fell to the Maple Leafs.

Most overtime goals by a player on a losing team, one series

2: Don Raleigh, NY Rangers, April 18 and 20, 1950
2: Joe Sakic, Colorado, April 28 and May 1, 2004

Without Gordie Howe, who was injured, Detroit still beat the Rangers, but it took seven games and three overtimes. Raleigh put New York up three games to two in the final series, with overtime winners in back-to-back games. But the Wings fought back with a 5–4 triumph in Game 6, then won Game 7 by a score of 4–3 when winger Pete Babando notched the Cup winner in double overtime. Raleigh's pair of overtime goals in 1950 went unmatched until John LeClair scored two in 1993's final. LeClair's goals counted for something though, as the Canadiens won the Cup. Joe Sakic bagged back-to-back overtime winners for Colorado in the 2004 playoffs against San Jose, but the Sharks prevailed in six games.

Most three-or-more goal games by players in losing causes, one series

2: Dale Hunter, Washington; Ray Ferraro, NY Islanders, 1993

Hunter and Ferraro are the only opposing players to score hat tricks in losing causes in one playoff round. Hunter's three goals took the Capitals into double overtime before a crushing 5–4 defeat by the Islanders on April 20, 1993. Six nights later, Washington paid back New York with six goals to take the shine off Ferraro, who scored all four goals in the 6–4 loss. The hard-fought six-game series featured three overtime matches, two in double OT.

Most three-or-more-goal games by a player who did not win a Cup, career

6: Dino Ciccarelli, 1981 to 1999

If Ciccarelli had a couple of Stanley Cup rings in his resumé, his status as a clutch player would rise a few notches. But even if the teams that he played for didn't win it all, he can't be blamed. His 73 playoff-goal tally leads all Cup-less players, as do his five three-goal games and one four-goal game.

Most three-or-more-goal games by a player who did not win a Cup, one playoff year

2: several players

Notching a pair of hat tricks in one playoff year is rare, and among those who've done it, the majority still couldn't turn that success into a Cup. Eight players with double hat tricks have gone Cup-less, including Wayne Gretzky in three postseasons: 1981, 1983 and 1997. Gretzky and Jari Kurri are the last playoff performers with at least two hat tricks in a Cup-winning year. They did it in 1985.

Most hat tricks by a player on a losing team, career

2: Steve Yzerman, Detroit, April 6, 1989 and May 8, 1996

What did Yzerman do to deserve this? Two of his four playoff hat tricks were recorded in 5–4 Detroit losses. Both came in overtime, to boot. The Red Wings were beaten by Chicago in 1989 and St. Louis in 1996.

First player to score a hat trick in a losing cause

Alf Skinner, Toronto Arenas, March 23, 1918

Skinner was the first NHLer to feel the frustration of losing a game after scoring a hat trick. Toronto was defeated 6–4 in Game 2 of the finals by the Vancouver Millionaires, but went on to win the five-game series and the NHL's first Stanley Cup championship. Skinner scored eight times to pace the Arenas.

Last player to score a hat trick in a loss during the finals and still win the Cup
Ted Kennedy, Toronto, April 14, 1945

It was the kind of wild playoff series few could have predicted. Toronto, the third-place team that finished 28 points back of Montreal, outgunned the defending Cup champion Canadiens in the semifinals. Then, they overwhelmed heavily favoured Detroit with three straight shutout wins in the finals. In Game 4, despite Ted Kennedy's hat trick, the Maple Leafs folded in the third period and lost 5–3. The series turned on that game, as the Red Wings rebounded with two straight shutouts, setting the stage for a Game 7 showdown in Detroit. The underdog Leafs edged the Wings 2–1, winning the Cup on a Babe Pratt goal in one of hockey's most unlikely championship series. Kennedy led all playoff marksmen with seven goals.

Most shutouts by a goalie who did not win a Cup, career
16: Curtis Joseph, 1989–90 to 2003–04

Only seven shutouts fewer than record holder Patrick Roy, and Joseph has never even been to the finals. Will he at least get the chance to be a bridesmaid at the big dance?

Most shutouts by a goalie who did not win a Cup, one playoff year
5: Jean-Sebastien Giguere, Anaheim, 2003
5: Miikka Kiprusoff, Calgary, 2004

Giguere put on a clinic for backstoppers in 2003. The playoff

MVP took the broom to Detroit in the first round, then defeated Dallas in six, swept Minnesota and pushed New Jersey to seven games before losing the Cup. Giguere blanked Dallas and New Jersey once and Minnesota in the first three games of the Conference finals. It was only the second time in history that a goalie opened a series with three straight zeros. In 2004, Kiprusoff matched Giguere's total in a losing cause for Calgary. The Finnish-born netminder recorded five zeros in 26 games.

Most shutouts by a losing goalie, one series
3: Turk Broda, Toronto, 1950
Broda actually posted four 60-minute shutout games in the 1950 semifinals. The only problem was that the Maple Leafs failed to score in Game 7, and Broda eventually lost both his goose egg and the series when Detroit's Leo Reise scored at 8:39 of sudden death.

CHAPTER 16

Silversmiths

Jack Darragh and Mike Bossy will forever be linked by one common fact. Never mind that they are both Hall of Famers who played right wing and won four Cups with their respective teams, Darragh and Bossy are the only players to score Cup winners in consecutive years. They did it more than 60 years apart: Darragh with Ottawa in 1920 and 1921 and Bossy with the Islanders in 1982 and 1983.

Most years in finals

12: *Maurice Richard, Montreal, 1944 to 1960*

12: *Red Kelly, Detroit (7), Toronto (5), 1948 to 1967*

12: *Jean Béliveau, Montreal, 1954 to 1971*

12: Henri Richard, Montreal, 1956 *to 1973*

This abundance of playoff experience helped win these four champions 37 Cups. Kelly is the only non-Montreal Canadien to win at least eight championships.

Most consecutive years in finals
10: Bernie Geoffrion, Montreal, 1951 to 1960
10: Doug Harvey, Montreal, 1951 to 1960
10: Tom Johnson, Montreal, 1951 to 1960
10: Bert Olmstead, Montreal, 1951 to 1958;
Toronto, 1959 and 1960

Montreal built its game around speed, and the team was branded with a style of play called firewagon hockey. This record looks unbeatable today. Imagine a present-day player going to the finals as often as these members of the Canadiens did between 1951 and 1960: 10 straight years.

Most consecutive games in finals, career

53: Bernie Geoffrion, Montreal, Game 1 in 1951 to Game 4 in 1960

48: Dickie Moore, Montreal, Game 1 in 1952 to Game 4 in 1960

Geoffrion is the only NHLer to play every finals game between 1951 and 1960. Boom-Boom led the Canadiens in final series scoring an amazing six times, recording 46 points in 53 straight games.

Fewest goals before scoring a Cup winner, career (since 1927)

0: Pete Kelly, Detroit, 1936
0: Mike Rupp, New Jersey, 2003

Kelly had just nine NHL goals and none in the playoffs before he scored the Cup winner in a 3–2 Detroit win over Toronto on April 11, 1936. Sixty-seven years later, Rupp matched the feat when his first playoff marker stood up as the Cup winner in New Jersey's 3–0 Game 7 win over Anaheim on June 9, 2003.

Fastest Cup-winning overtime goal

40 seconds: Bobby Orr, Boston, May 10, 1970

It's not only the fastest, it may be also be the most famous, thanks to a stirring Ray Lussier photo of Orr flying through the air after he put the puck past St. Louis Blues goalie Glenn Hall.

Only player to score a Cup-winning goal on a two-man-advantage

Bill Cook, NY Rangers, April 13, 1933

Whew, they must have officiated games a lot differently in the 1930s. The Rangers knocked off Toronto 1–0 when Cook scored at 7:33 of overtime after the Leafs received two minors: the first to Alex Levinsky for tripping; the second to Bill Thoms for accidentally knocking the puck over the boards near centre ice.

Age of youngest player to score a Cup-winning goal

21.4 years: Ted Kennedy, Toronto, 1947
21.6 years: Alex Tanguay, Colorado, 2001

Dubbed the Leaflets because they were the NHL's youngest team, the 1946–47 Maple Leafs beat Montreal in six games during the finals on a goal by 21-year-old Kennedy. Tanguay was just two months older than Kennedy when he notched the Avalanche's Cup winner in 2001.

Most penalty minutes, one finals series

53: Mel Bridgman, Philadelphia, 1980
49: Chris Nilan, Montreal, 1986

Bridgman captained the Flyers to the 1980 finals but couldn't stay out of the penalty box. He amassed a total of 70 minutes during 19 playoff games that year, but a record 53 minutes came during six games against the New York Islanders in the finals. By comparison, Gordie Howe, the all-time leader, only recorded 94 minutes in 55 Cup finals games. Nilan did his best to top Bridgman, but didn't see enough ice time. He racked up 49 PIM in just three games in the 1986 finals.

Most Cup-winning goals allowed by a goalie, career
6: Glenn Hall, 1955 to 1971

Although this record doesn't call for bragging, it proves the calibre of play Hall demonstrated game in and game out in the NHL. Few teams would give a goalie so many opportunities at losing a Cup. In fact, in Hall's case, he was so good that three teams afforded him the honour of backstopping them in the finals. He gave up Cup winners with Detroit in 1956; with Chicago in 1962 and 1965, and with St. Louis in 1968, 1969 and 1970. Hall won one Cup with Chicago in 1961.

Only goalie supposedly recruited from a tavern for a Cup finals game

Alfie Moore, Chicago, April 5, 1938

Moore's story of being half-soused when he was hauled out of a tavern to play as a fill-in goalie during a Cup finals game is the stuff of legend. Unfortunately, it's not true. Moore, a minor-leaguer who lived in Toronto, was indeed called the day of Game 1

of the 1938 finals, but he wasn't drinking at a tavern, he was
at home. His instructions were to be at Maple Leafs Gardens by
6 PM, where he would be starting for Chicago as a replacement
for an injured Mike Karakas. That night, Moore played his heart
out in front of a hometown crowd and defeated the Maple Leafs
3–1. Chicago went on to win the Cup in four games. Moore's finest
NHL hour became legend, but from then on, he faced a lifetime
of grief on each and every visit to the Gardens.

Most Cup-clinching games by a winning goalie, career
6: Ken Dryden, 1971 to 1979
Dryden was in goal each time the Montreal Canadiens won the
Cup between 1971 and 1979. Fellow Canadiens goalie Jacques
Plante also won six Cups, but he was only in the nets for five
Cup victories from 1956 to 1960. Gerry McNeil was between the
pipes for Montreal's Cup win in 1953.

First masked goalie to win the Cup
Jacques Plante, Montreal, April 14, 1960
Plante introduced his mask on November 1, 1959, then wore it
the rest of the season and throughout the playoffs. Montreal
claimed its record fifth consecutive Cup, but it was the first by a
goalie donning face protection. The second Cup-winning goalie
to wear a mask was Toronto's Don Simmons, subbing for an
injured Johnny Bower in 1962.

Last goalie without a mask to win the Cup
Gump Worsley, Montreal, May 4, 1969
It's an interesting twist of fate that the last maskless goalie to
win the Cup played on the same team wearing the same sweater
number as the first masked man to win the Cup. Nine years after
Plante's historic first on April 14, 1960, Worsley played the last

Cup-winning game by a barefaced netminder. The next year, when Boston won the championship, Gerry Cheevers was sporting his famous white mask with the stitch marks. From that point on, all Cup-winning goalies wore face protection.

Most shutouts in Cup-winning games

2: Clint Benedict, Ottawa, 1923; Montreal Maroons, 1926
2: Bernie Parent, Philadelphia, 1974 and 1975
Had the Conn Smythe Trophy been around in Benedict's day, he would have certainly been named playoff MVP of several finals. Benedict beat the Edmonton Eskimos 1–0 in Game 6 of the 1923 finals; and, as a Maroon, defeated the Victoria Cougars 2–0 in Game 4 of the 1926 finals. Parent, who earned consecutive MVP awards, defeated Boston 1–0 in Game 6 of the 1974 finals; and Buffalo 2–0 in Game 6 of the 1975 finals.

Most misspelled name on the Cup

Jacques Plante, Montreal
Poor Plante. The Montreal goalie won six Cups between 1953 and 1960 and four times the engraver spelled his name wrong. The mistakes included Jocko, Jack, Jacq and Plant.

First player to have the spelling of his name corrected on the Cup

Adam Deadmarsh, Colorado, 1996
The NHL broke with its long tradition of not correcting an engraver's mistakes on the Cup when it amended the spelling of Deadmarch to Deadmarsh in 1996. A second correction was made in 2002, when Detroit's Manny Lagece was changed to Legace.

First woman to have her name engraved on the Cup
Lily Murphy, 1911

Someone pulled a few strings. Lily Murphy's husband, Dennis, whose name is also on the Cup, was president of the Bank of Ottawa when the original Ottawa Senators won the Cup in 1911. After Murphy, the next woman to have her name engraved on the trophy was Detroit Red Wings president Marguerite Norris, in 1955.

Only dog to get his name on the Cup
Bow-Wow, Quebec Bulldogs, 1912, 1913

Every dog has its day. But Bow-Wow had a couple of them in 1912 and 1913, when he got his name etched on the Cup. Unfortunately, no one knows for sure exactly who Bow-Wow was. Hockey historians speculate that he may have been the mascot of the Cup-winning Quebec Bulldogs or a pet of one of the players.

Most popular player's family name on the Cup
Smith

Fourteen different Smiths have had their names engraved on the Cup a total of 25 times. Billy Smith leads with four Cup engravings for the New York Islanders from 1980 to 1983—and he is only one of two goalies named Smith to backstop Cup winners. Normie Smith captured Cups with Detroit in 1936 and 1937. Hooley Smith is the only Smith to win the Cup with two different teams (the Ottawa Senators in 1927 and the Montreal Maroons in 1935). There have also been Smiths on Boston's last three Cup winners: Des Smith in 1941 and Dallas and Rick Smith in 1970 and 1972.

Most finals coached
16: Dick Irvin, 1931 to 1955
13: Scotty Bowman, 1968 to 2002

Irvin survived longer than anyone but won only four Cups. He coached
Montreal in eight finals, Toronto in seven and Chicago in one, winning
once with the Maple Leafs and three times with Montreal. Bowman
coached more teams to the finals than any other bench boss: five
with Montreal, four with Detroit, three with St. Louis and one with
Pittsburgh.

Most wins in the finals by a coach, career
36: Scotty Bowman, 1968 to 2002
34: Toe Blake, 1956 to 1968
32: Dick Irvin, 1931 to 1955

All three coaches earned most of their wins behind the bench
of the Montreal Canadiens. Bowman coached the Canadiens to
20 finals wins, Detroit to 12 and Pittsburgh to four. Bowman's
mentor, Toe Blake, recorded all 34 victories with Montreal's
dynasty teams of the 1950s and 1960s. Irvin, who preceded
Blake, had 21 wins with Montreal, nine with Toronto and
two with Chicago.

First coach suspended during a Cup finals
Jack Adams, Detroit, 1942

Adams picked a bad time to lose it. His Red Wings were leading
Toronto three games to one in the finals and already planning
their victory party, when the shape of the series abruptly
changed in Game 4. Incensed by the calls of referee Mel Hard-
wood, which he believed had helped Toronto to win 4–3, Adams
and several of his players accosted the ref as he was leaving the

ice. Punches were thrown and NHL president Frank Calder, who was at the game, suspended Adams for the rest of the series. The Red Wings unravelled without their coach, and the Leafs swept the next three games to win the Cup.

First NHL coaches to meet in a Cup finals who were former teammates
Jack Adams and Hap Day, 1942
Adams and Day played together on the Toronto St. Pats for two years, in 1924–25 and 1925–26. They met as combatants in the 1942 finals, with Day's Maple Leafs beating Adams's Red Wings in seven games.

First NHL coaches to meet in a Cup finals who also played against one another in a Cup finals
Toe Blake and Milt Schmidt, 1957
Blake of the Canadiens and Schmidt of the Bruins were fierce rivals, first as players and then as coaches. They squared off on the ice in the 1946 finals, a series won by Montreal in five games, then clashed in 1957 and 1958 as bench bosses, with Blake's Flying Frenchmen winning both times.

First coach to defeat his former coach in a Cup finals
Hap Day, Toronto, 1947
When Day's Maple Leafs downed Dick Irvin's Canadiens in the 1947 finals, it was a case of the mentor toppling his teacher. Day had been captain of the Irwin-coached Maple Leafs in the 1930s. But that's not the only time a coach defeated his former coach in a Cup finals. Four years later, another of Irvin's former players, Joe Primeau, coached Toronto to the Cup in 1951, defeating Irwin's Canadiens. As well, Montreal coach Al MacNeil, who had played under Billy Reay in Chicago in the 1960s, defeated his

mentor in the 1971 finals. And Jacques Lemaire won the Cup with New Jersey in 1995, sweeping the Red Wings, who were led by Lemaire's former Montreal boss Scotty Bowman.

Most inspirational move by a coach to motivate his players

Playing goalie: Lester Patrick, NY Rangers, April 7, 1928

Rangers coach Lester Patrick donned the bloodstained pads of injured goalie Lorne Chabot and stepped into the crease for the second half of Game 2 of the 1928 finals against the Montreal Maroons. The 44-year-old Patrick gave up just one goal and held off the Maroons in overtime until Frank Boucher scored for New York in the 2–1 thriller, "ending Patrick's anguish. His players mobbed him as he left the ice and it appeared nothing could hold the Rangers now," reported Charles L. Coleman in *The Trail of the Stanley Cup*. Montreal won once more but couldn't stop the Rangers, who took Game 4 and 5 to capture the best-of-five series and the Cup in only their second NHL season.

First team to use oxygen on the bench

Detroit Red Wings, April 16, 1949

Trailing Toronto three games to none in the 1949 Stanley Cup finals, Red Wings coach Tommy Ivan tried a last-gasp tactic to turn the tide. He borrowed tanks of oxygen from the Eastern Canada junior champion Montreal Royals and had his players inhale the stuff on the bench during Game 4. The gimmick had no discernible effect. The Leafs prevailed 3–1 and took the Cup.

Most goalies used by one team, one finals series

3: New York Rangers, 1928
3: Chicago Blackhawks, 1938
3: St Louis Blues, 1970

In 1928, New York used Lorne Chabot, Lester Patrick and Joe

Miller to beat Montreal; in 1938, Chicago went with Mike Karakas, Alfie Moore and Paul Goodman to defeat Toronto; and in 1970, St. Louis dressed Jacques Plante, Glenn Hall and Ernie Wakely in its series loss to Boston. Interestingly, among the three teams, the club with regular backup goalies, St. Louis, lost its Cup, while the two teams that had to scramble for replacements when their only goalie got injured, won their championships. Of course, neither the 1928 Rangers nor the 1938 Blackhawks had to face St. Louis' finals foe: Bobby Orr and the Bruins.

Most rookies to play for two teams, one finals series
18: Montreal Canadiens vs. Calgary Flames, 1986
Youth carried the Canadiens and Flames to the 1986 finals. Montreal iced 10 freshmen and Calgary played eight. Even the two opposing goalies—Patrick Roy and Mike Vernon—were rookies. Montreal won in five games.

Most consecutive series losses in the Cup finals
3: Toronto Maple Leafs, 1938, 1939, 1940
3: St. Louis Blues, 1968, 1969, 1970
Two teams have gone to the big dance and been jilted three straight times: Toronto and, most recently, St. Louis, who lost to Montreal in 1968 and 1969, then to Boston in 1970.

Most wins by a team in its first playoffs
12: Florida Panthers, 1996
Most teams get kicked in the head when they graduate to the playoffs for the first time, but Florida surprised everyone in its first trip to the postseason in 1996. Spurred on by

plastic-rat-throwing fans, the Panthers knocked off Boston, Philadelphia and then Mario Lemieux and the Pittsburgh Penguins in the first three playoff rounds. But their luck ran out in the finals as the Colorado Avalanche streamrolled the Floridians in four straight games.

Most division winners eliminated by a Cup finalist
3: Calgary Flames, 2004

No team has ever taken such a tough route to the big dance. In the first playoff round, the Flames outlasted Vancouver, the Northwest Division champs, in a seven-game thriller. In round two, they conquered Detroit, the Central Division winners, in six gruelling games. In the third round, the Flames eliminated San Jose, the Pacific Division champs, in six tightly contested games. Then in the finals, Calgary met its fourth divisional champion and the Eastern Conference's top-seeded team, the Tampa Bay Lightning. This time, the Flames ran out of gas, going down to defeat in seven bone-grinding contests.

Last defunct team to win the Cup
Montreal Maroons, 1935

NHL history is littered with the wreckage of failed franchises. In 13 years the Maroons won the Cup twice. Their first triumph came in 1926, the last year that teams outside the NHL were able to compete for the Cup, when they beat the Victoria Cougars in the finals. The Maroons won the Cup again in 1935, defeating Toronto in three straight games. They folded after 1937–38, but retain the distinction of being the last defunct NHL team to win Lord Stanley's trophy.

Most consecutive years with a different Cup-winning team

6: 1931 to 1936; and 1992 to 1997

Only twice in NHL history have six different teams managed to capture the Cup in consecutive years. Between 1931 and 1936, the Cup was won by Montreal, Toronto, Detroit, Chicago, the New York Rangers and the Montreal Maroons. Sixty-one years later it happened again, between 1992 and 1997, with Pittsburgh, Montreal, New Jersey, Detroit, Colorado and the Rangers all taking home the big prize.

Most unfavourable site for a Stanley Cup parade

A parking lot in New Jersey, 1995

With no real city to stage a parade in, the Devils celebrated their 1995 Cup win outside Meadowlands Arena in the rink's parking lot. It may have been the ultimate tailgate party, but still, the festivities lacked the spectacle of a big downtown parade.

Most unusual place for a team engraving on the Cup

Inside the Cup's bowl

The charm of the Stanley Cup lies not just in its legacy but in its inconsistencies. Attempts to standardize the engravings only began in the 1930s; earlier teams often chose where to put their names. A few teams favoured the inside of the bowl (a choice site that few get to view unless it is through champagne). The bottom is engraved with "Wanderers defeated Kenora, 12 to 8, March 25th, 1907" and the names of the Wanderers players. And along the walls of the bowl, the fluting is engraved with the names of the 1915 Vancouver Millionaires.

ACKNOWLEDGEMENTS

Thanks to the following for the use of statistical and anecdotal material:

- *The Official NHL Guide and Record Book,* various years
- *Total Hockey, Total Stanley Cup, Total NHL* and *Years of Glory* by Dan Diamond and Associates, Inc.
- *The Trail of the Stanley Cup* by Charles H. Coleman
- *The Rules of Hockey* by James Duplacey
- *Players: The Ultimate A–Z Guide* and *The Detroit Red Wings Book* by Andrew Podnieks
- *The Hockey Compendium* by Jeff Z. Klein and Karl-Eric Reif
- *Ultimate Hockey* by Glenn Weir, Jeff Chapman and Travis Weir
- *The Hockey News Century of Hockey,* edited by Steve Dryden
- *In the Crease* and *Behind the Bench* by Dick Irvin
- *A Breed Apart* by Douglas Hunter
- *Grace under Fire* by Lawrence Scanlan
- *Pavel Bure: The Riddle of the Russian Rocket* by Kerry Banks
- *Overtime: The Legend of Guy Lafleur* by Georges-Hebert Germain
- *Mario* by Lawrence Martin
- *Boom-Boom* by Bernard Geoffrion and Stan Fischler
- *Gordie: A Hockey Legend* by Roy MacSkimming
- *Gordie Howe: My Hockey Memories* by Gordie Howe
- *Our Life with the Rocket* by Roch Carrier
- *The Leafs, The Habs, The Rangers, The Bruins, The Hawks* and *The Red Wings* by Brian McFarlane
- *What's the Score?* by Liam McGuire

- *Hockey Shorts* by Glenn Liebman
- *Hockey's Home: Halifax–Dartmouth—The Origin of Canada's Game* by Martin Jones
- *Same Game, Different Name* by Jack Lautier and Frank Polnaszek
- *The Unofficial Guide* series by Don Weekes and Kerry Banks

Also, we are indebted to *The Hockey News;* several Web sites, including *hockeydb.ca, faceoff.com, shrpsports.com, NHL.com, hhof.com;* the *Globe and Mail* archives at *globeandmail.com;* and *Sports Illustrated, Faceoff, the National Post, Globe and Mail, Vancouver Sun* and *Montreal Gazette.*

Thanks to the following for their use of quoted material:
- From *The Game I'll Never Forget* by Chris McDonell. Published by Firefly Books Ltd.
- *Gretzky: An Autobiography* by Wayne Gretzky with Rick Reilly. Published by HarperCollins Publishers Ltd.
- *The Miami Herald.* Published by Knight Ridder.

The authors gratefully acknowledge the help of everyone at *The Hockey News;* Gary Meagher and Benny Ercolani of the NHL; Phil Pritchard at the Hockey Hall of Fame; the staff at the McLellan-Redpath Library at McGill University; Rob Sanders, Susan Rana and Chris Labonte at Greystone Books; the many hockey writers, broadcast journalists, media and Internet organization staff who have made the game better through their own work; Cathy Newton for stat-checking; as well as editor Anne Rose, typesetter Bonne Zabolotney and designer Peter Cocking for their patience, dedication and expertise.

PLAYER, COACH AND GM INDEX

Halko, Steve, 109
Hall, Glenn, 2, 23, 84, 91, 209, 210, 217
Hamilton, Jack, 58, 62–63
Harkness, Ned, 118
Hart, Gizzy, 19
Harvey, Doug, 4, 46, 143, 208
Hasek, Dominik, 68, 85
Hayes, Chris, 179
Healy, Glenn, 154
Hedberg, Johan, 82
Heinze, Steve, 18, 159
Hejduk, Milan, 63
Henderson, John, 93
Henderson, Paul, 11
Henry, Jim, 95
Herron, Denis, 91
Hextall Jr., Bryan, 45
Hextall Sr., Bryan, 124
Hextall, Ron, 143
Hickie, Ernie, 173
Hill, Mel, 194
Hitchman, Lionel, 22
Hodge, Ken, 117, 149
Holden, Mark, 136
Holik, Bobby, 132
Holland, Ken, 68
Holland, Robbie, 136
Holmes, Hap, 92, 182
Holmgren, Paul, 146, 157
Horner, Red, 6, 38
Horton, Nathan, 62
Horton, Tim, 24, 71

Hospodar, Ed, 45
Houle, Réjean, 132–133, 138
Housley, Phil, 130, 174
Howe, Gordie, 4–5, 14, 28, 30, 39, 46, 53, 59, 60, 73, 76, 101, 106, 108–109, 153, 182, 195, 203, 210
Howe, Syd, 26, 62
Howe, Vic, 109
Howell, Harry, 182
Hrudey, Kelly, 61
Hull, Bobby, 14, 15, 153, 195, 200
Hull, Brett, 18, 67–68, 100–101, 102–103, 108, 126, 157, 161, 164
Hunter, Dale, 40, 133, 198, 202, 203
Hyland, Harry, 60

I

Iafrate, Al, 162
Imlach, Punch, 111, 136, 144–145
Irbe, Arturs, 118
Ironstone, Joe, 89
Irvin, Dick, 110, 112, 114, 144, 145, 146, 149, 214, 215
Ivan, Tommy, 216

J

Jackson, Don, 142–143
Jagr, Jaromir, 18, 69, 76, 124
James, Gerry, 185
Jenkins, Roger, 21
Johnson, Matt, 49
Johnson, Tom, 46, 146, 208